JUST DO IT!

My Personal Testimony

DANNY ABER

Just Do IT!

My Personal Testimony

DANNY ABER

ISBN 1-931600-28-7

Copyright© 1996 by Danny K. Aber
All rights reserved
All Scripture quotations in this book are from the King James Version of the Bible.

No portion of this publication may be reproduced in any form, without the prior permission and written consent of the author.

Additional copies may be ordered from the copyright holder.

Copyright holder:
Danny K. Aber
2632 Slide Canyon Ave.
North Las Vegas, NV 89081

Acknowledgements

everend M.J. Moore, my pastor, who taught me to love souls.

To my wife, Lori, who is my completer. I love you so much. I could not do anything without your Christian example of love. Your commitment to reaching the lost has forever challenged me.

To my son, Ryan, who has traveled to Costa Rica, Panama, Guyana and Suriname with me and has always been a blessing.

To my daughter, Leslie Victoria, my traveling partner, always ready to go up the river and make some new friends.

To my mother, for her encouragement to put my testimony on paper.

To all the souls who have remained in this truth who are mentioned in this book.

Dedication

*This publication is dedicated to my family:
Lori, Ryan, and Leslie Victoria.
I love you.*

Contents

FOREWORD ix

INTRODUCTION xi

Chapter 1
The Party's Over! 1

Chapter 2
You Gotta Serve Somebody 15

Chapter 3
Radical Adjustments to Extreme Dilemmas 23

Chapter 4
Aber's God Is Tough 29

Chapter 5
The Consequences of Divine Exposure 35

Chapter 6
Thank You, Devil, Five Souls 45

Chapter 7
His Harvest 53

Chapter 8
Don't Leave Home Without It 63

Chapter 9
The Need of Divine Help 69

Chapter 10
Just Do It 75

Foreword

ark 16:15, "And he said unto them, Go ye into all the world, and preach the gospel to every creature."

Just prior to Jesus ascending into heaven, He gave His disciples His last instructions to "go ye...."

"Go" are the first two letters of the word Gospel. He wants us to go everywhere and tell everyone about Jesus.

Think about that. Everywhere we go we are to be a witness and share the goodness of God. How many people do we pass by everyday and decide that we just don't have the time to share the good news?

Pastor Aber's book *JUST DO IT!* will challenge you to become the witness that Jesus wants you to be. Oftentimes Christians feel intimidated by today's society and then carry guilt for not being the witness God wants them to be. Pastor Aber gives us a simple clear-cut plan to fulfill God's mission in our lives. His title *JUST DO IT!* says it all.

My personal testimony is very much like Brother Aber's. I was involved in satanism, witchcraft, seances and hypnotism. I was involved in them trying to find the purpose of

God in my life. I remember hearing the voice of God calling me to Him long before I was able to receive the Spirit. As I look back I can see God's hand was clearly on my life. When the voice I could hear in my head and feel in my heart led me to the path of a young and zealous Christian, I was ready to receive. Pastor Chester Wright was the vessel that God used. He knocked on my door, witnessed to me, and led me to the truth. I am so thankful that Pastor Wright was obedient to the Word and was preaching the Gospel to everyone. He had the "Go" in Gospel.

My new convert days were similar to Brother Aber's. I witnessed to everything that moved. As a milkman I made up my mind to witness to every customer on my route and touch their lives. Many of them came to the house of God. Even today there are saints in Brother Wright's church that I brought into the Kingdom, with the help of the Lord, 25 years ago. Over the years I have grown in wisdom and knowledge, but still have a burden for the lost. God continues to show me ways He deals with people as He brings them to the house of God and in my personal pathway.

Pastor Aber's work in Texas, as well as various mission fields, has proven how seriously he takes the commandment to go into all the world and preach the Gospel to every creature. Having recently returned from the General Conference in Guyana, South America, and in three nights seeing 70 filled with the Spirit, watching his burden and his zeal has convinced me that he knows a little bit about how to preach and teach. This book will be a blessing to you and to those with whom you share it. My hat is off to Pastor Aber and the work that he is doing and I congratulate him for this book. I want to "go" more than I've ever gone before. God bless you.

Sincerely,
Pastor R.E. Libby
Pastor of Christian Life Center
Gaithersburg, Maryland

Introduction

Gathered Fragments

John 6:12, *"...Gather up the fragments that remain, that nothing be lost."*

The purpose of this book is to help everyone understand that Jesus still intends for us to gather up the fragments.

The world is getting worse and worse. Everyday newspapers carry the news of another murder, tragedy or war. It seems that divorce is at an all-time high and single parenting has become the norm. Marijuana, cocaine, and heroin are very popular and teen pregnancy and abortion still chip away at the very moral foundation of America. All these problems result in broken things, or fragments.

Jesus cares for broken things. He cares for the broken hearts, the broken lives and the broken families. It is His desire for us to gather up the fragments or broken things, that none be lost or wasted.

My life was fragmented in many ways. The loss of my father and my job caused me to give up hope. I was ready to end it all until April 9, 1980, when I was gathered up with some other fragmented lives. I am thankful that someone took the time to gather up the fragments of my life so that I would not be lost.

It is my desire that you find within these pages something that inspires you to look at people differently, and to understand their need of a life-changing experience, and then a personal relationship with Jesus Christ.

Gather up the fragments, so none will be lost.

1

The Party's Over!

I was born and raised in El Campo, Texas, a small town southwest of Houston. I graduated from El Campo High School in 1974 and decided not to go to college, but to work in the oil fields as a roughneck instead.

Over the next four years, I experienced many difficulties in my life. I experimented with drugs and eventually reached the point where I needed them to function each day.

My drug problem became so severe that I changed jobs at least 30 times and lived in ten different cities during these four years.

I found myself slipping further away from reality. Suicide was always a thought lingering in my messed up mind. My life was slowly deteriorating, and I knew I was in need of a drastic change. I felt I had finally hit rock bottom.

I was living in an old rustic country shack on top of a hill near Canyon Lake, Texas, with two other guys, Cleve and Greg. Cleve, who was the owner of the house, raised fighting cocks and marijuana. Greg and I worked for the Southwest Harvesters Company out of New Braunfels.

One night we drove to Bandera, Texas, and went to the Purple Cow, a dance hall where Willie Nelson was singing. Cleve's father was playing in Nelson's band that night, and we went to see him. After the dance, he invited us to his hotel room where we smoked pot, drank and partied for most of the night. We were having what the world calls a good time. Even though getting high was my way to gain friends and cope with my insecurities, I'll never forget how out of place I felt that night. I was trying to find myself, but was getting further away from reality.

On June 3, 1978, my boss and I had an argument on the job, and because I lost my temper, I quit. For the next two days I sat around the house smoking pot and feeling sorry for myself. With thoughts of suicide on my mind again, I decided to get high and watch a movie called *Kelly's Heroes.* It was a World War II comedy about some crazy, Army guys in a tank having fun smoking dope. As I watched, stoned out of my mind, I made a decision that I felt would get me out of my dilemma. I had a brainstorm! I would join the Army and be just like the tank commander in the movie.

The very next day I went to the Army recruiter in Seguin, Texas. I was stoned as I walked through the doors of his office. Broke, hungry, and not too proud at the moment, I told the recruiter I would join the Army if he would buy me a steak.

He pulled out the paperwork, made the necessary phone calls, and set up my testing for the next day in San Antonio. We then left his office in search of a steak house.

The following day I arrived at the AFEE's building in San Antonio. There must have been 100 other young men there. We were herded around like cattle from one station to the next for most of the day.

After the testing, we were moved into a room where we signed up for our M.O.S., or job description. This is where they let you pick out the job they want you to have. I requested to be in Armour (tanks) and lucky for me a high test score was not one of the qualifications needed for that job. There was also a $2,500 bonus upon completion of that

M.O.S., but the truth of the matter was, I figured I would rather ride in a tank than walk.

We were led into a room where we raised our right hand and took an oath. Officially, I was now in the U.S. Army. They asked me when I wanted to leave for basic training (boot camp) and my reply was, "As soon as possible."

Three days later, I had a room at the Gunner Hotel, just up the street from the Alamo, gratis Uncle Sam. Shortly after check-in, I met some other young men who were also leaving the next morning. We decided to walk to the walls of the Alamo and smoke the last of my bag of dope. Early the next day, I was on an airplane headed for Fort Knox, Kentucky.

Arriving at the fort about two o'clock in the morning was a real bummer. We were met by a drill instructor who was obviously upset with someone, probably us for coming in at such an hour. He yelled at us for the first 30 minutes, and then emptied each of our bags on the floor in front of us looking for drugs and other paraphernalia. After the inspection, he finally calmed down. I was relieved to know he had a normal voice, but it did not last long. He zeroed in on me standing there about 30 pounds overweight, with this huge afro and bloodshot eyes. I was definitely not material for the next "Be All You Can Be in the Army" poster. He stood about six inches from my face, and again used his loud voice to ask, "Where are you from?"

I replied, "Texas."

He went ballistic.

"You mean to tell me you came all the way from Texas just to make me mad!" he screamed.

Immediately, I began to have second thoughts about my reasons for joining the Army. This was nothing like the movie I had seen a week earlier. I also remembered that I had joined the Army so that no one could tell me what to do. I realized that if something did not change, it was going to be a very long 14 weeks.

The next day they marched us through the various stations, giving us our clothes, testing our eyes and hearing, teaching us how to brush our teeth (a very humbling experience), and they even shaved our heads and charged us $1.50 for the haircut. It did not take us long to find out that no one had rights in the Army. You became the property of Uncle Sam as soon as you arrived. He told you when to eat, when to sleep, when to wake up, and even when to use the rest room.

During the afternoon break, I went to my room and grabbed the small New Testament Bible I had picked up at the AFEE's building in San Antonio. Walking outside away from everyone else, I sat down under a tree and started crying. I turned to the back of the little Bible and found the topic "loneliness" (it seemed appropriate for the moment). I promised myself not to let this opportunity to straighten out my life pass me by.

I began basic training with a good attitude. This was a major accomplishment, because I was one confused young man. I was still determined to find myself and make some things right.

My drill sergeants, Lumply and Toth, informed me that I was assigned to the Charlie Company, located at the Disney Barracks. They both seemed to enjoy playing with our minds. It was Sergeant Toth that scared me the most. His right arm was in a cast from an accident, but he still met us with a smile and told us that he was our physical training instructor. He yelled, "I won't ever ask you to do anything that I can't do." Needless to say, we were beside ourselves because the most popular exercise and punishment in the Army was push-ups. About the time he felt we were all thinking the same thing (no push-ups), he ordered, "On your stomachs!" We were all shocked, except for Sergeant Toth. He dropped to a front leaning rest position (push-up position) using only his left arm. He began to holler, "Up, down. Up, down. Up, down." He continued this until we were all exhausted laying on our stomachs. He then apologized because he was right-handed and could only do about 100 push-ups with his left arm.

Before we were allowed to enter the mess hall, they made us do push-ups, chin-ups and the crab crawl. Then we had to stand in line sweating, waiting for chow. As I was waiting to be served after that first morning of basic training, I could smell the bacon and eggs cooking. While anticipating a good meal, I heard someone call my name. Slowly turning in the direction of the voice, I saw my D.I. approaching me yelling loud enough for everyone to hear, "Aber, don't even think about bacon and eggs! Fat boys don't eat bacon and eggs. Fat boys eat grapefruit." He put two grapefruits on my plate and said, "Service with a smile." After three weeks of grapefruit and other fat-free meals, my weight dropped from 225 pounds to 186 pounds. I was now a lean, mean, fighting machine.

The next 11 weeks went by fast and I found myself standing at the front of the line during graduation. I won the Armour Association Award, the Outstanding Soldier Award, and was the Platoon Leader for the Honor Patrol. That was one of the greatest days of my life. I had finally become the best at something. I thought that surely this would make people respect me.

After graduation, I was promoted to acting corporal and was asked to remain in Fort Knox and be a tank commander for the next training session. I was now on top, and felt that nothing could stop me.

I soon found myself in a very strange situation. I could not handle the added pressure of my new responsibilities. I began to run with some of the older soldiers I now worked with and soon I was back to drinking and smoking dope.

I just could not seem to do right, no matter how hard I tried. I became very frustrated and once again began to think of suicide. It was a mystery to me why I could not stop using drugs. I had done so well in a confined environment, but once I was on my own I fell back into the same old rut.

After 14 weeks of living a lie and trying not to get caught using drugs, my orders for Germany finally came through. I found myself making promises to God, and trying to convince Him, and myself, that this time things would be different. This was going to be my new start. But little did I know that I was headed for the worst year of my life.

I chose Germany because that was where my father spent his time while in the service. I guess I was trying to get his approval because of all the disappointment I had caused him.

When I arrived in Frankfurt, Germany, I was amazed at the weeping willow trees, colorful flowers, beautiful parks, and the enchanting castles. Germany was one of the most beautiful places I had ever seen. But as I approached the old Hitler Barracks in Frieburg, I could feel the oppression around the concern (fort). I stood outside the building looking up at the four stories, and I asked myself, "Aber, what have you got yourself into this time?" I soon realized I was not going to make good on yet another promise.

I was assigned to the Third Armour Division, Headquarters Company. After meeting my company commander, I was taken to the fourth floor, first room on the right, and was introduced to the soldiers with whom I would be working and living. The room was set up for six soldiers, but there would be ten of us now that I had arrived.

After they all greeted me, Lloyd Wayland calmly asked, "Do you get high?"

I quickly replied, "NO!"

He laughed and with a wicked smile, said, "You will."

About two days later, I found myself in the room alone with Lloyd, who was fixing a bowl of hash. As that same wicked smile crossed his face, he tempted, saying, "Come over and join me." He added, "I drive the first sergeant around and they're all in a meeting. He gave me the rest of the day off."

Nothing else needed to be said. I pulled up a chair and broke another promise. I not only started using drugs, but Lloyd and I also started selling them.

During the next ten months of Army life, I cannot remember one night when I went to bed sober. I was either high on dope or drunk on alcohol. I was always lying to myself saying, "I'm all right, I'm in control."

Another roommate of mine, Rick Blommer, became my best friend. We were always getting high, going to rock concerts, to the Yes Club, and everywhere else. He was the only one who seemed to understand me. If it was not for Rick stopping me from doing some of the stupid things I planned, I might be dead or in prison today.

Our room was a gathering place where everyone got together. We always had loud rock music, beer, and plenty of dope.

Everyone in our room managed to get along with me, except Phillip Hooker. He was a dedicated G.I. Joe type, starch-ironed uniform, spit-shined boots and a bed you could bounce a quarter off of upon inspection. Phillip was your basic South Carolina redneck, who liked to drink beer and smoke Marlboro cigarettes. His great ambition in life was to go to Mickey Gilley's Club and ride the mechanical, bucking bull. He was the gung ho Army type, but he was no match for me. It took me a while, but I finally got to Phillip.

One night we were all sitting around playing cards, smoking hash, and drinking beer, when an idea came to me. Phillip was sitting on his bunk by himself, as usual, smoking a cigarette, and I decided to mess with his mind. We were all on speed and partying hard, so I put some speed in a can of beer and called for Phillip to join us. He declined, knowing that I was probably up to something. I kept on telling him that it was time we became friends, and eventually it got to him. I told him we were all going to down a whole can of beer as a token of friendship.

I was sitting there holding two cans of beer, one with the speed in it and the other one without. Knowing that he would think I was pulling a trick on him, I handed him the can of beer without the speed. Phillip laughed, and proclaimed his superior wit, stating, "Aber, I'm no fool, you put something in that can. Give me the other one!" I gladly did this and he downed it.

About ten minutes later, he was laying on his bed when all of the sudden he jumped up and opened his wall locker and stared into it for a few seconds, shut it, and lay back down. Two minutes later, he did the same thing and then he came over to our card game and asked if anyone wanted to go to Frankfurt. "I feel a little restless, kind of nervous," he said.

We all laughed and declined to go to town with Phillip. We were laughing because we noticed that he was talking faster than normal and realized the speed had taken effect. We all had a big laugh at Phillip's expense.

He was out all night walking the streets of Frankfurt, trying to figure out what was wrong. The sad thing was, Phillip's life had begun to be ruined also.

About six weeks later, I convinced Phillip to smoke hash with us. We were sitting around my living area watching *Saturday Night Live* on TV when all of a sudden, TOP (our First Sergeant) walked in.

We had just finished smoking two bowls of hash and we were all stoned out of our minds. Everyone was a veteran drug user and knew how to act, except Phillip. We remained calm and kept watching TV, but Phillip ran to the window, opened it and stuck his head out into 30 degree weather. Of course, TOP thought that was pretty strange and asked Phillip what was wrong. Phillip was so paranoid he totally lost it. Unable to respond, he bumped into the wall locker and then tripped over a rug. He then tried to run out of the room, but was unable to open the door the first few tries. I thought for sure it was over for us. But TOP, knowing that Phillip was a good soldier, thought he was just drunk and nothing else was said. We escaped being busted once again.

Not long after that incident I introduced Phillip to LSD. We watched him get messed up and then we left him alone. He was at the movie theater when it started playing with his mind. He ran out screaming, and then ran around the football field about four times. Once back at the room he began to lose it again. He said the pictures on the walls started moving, so he ran out looking for me. But this time he almost lost his life. Phillip ran out into traffic in front of the concern, hollering, "Aber, where are you?" Cars started screeching to a stop after they swerved to miss him. All this excitement got the attention of a sergeant who was off duty. He grabbed Phillip from the middle of the road and took him back to his room and sat with him until we returned. I must say again I was very lucky because the sergeant who found Phillip was a drug user also. He knew me and understood what was going on and overlooked the matter.

After thinking I had destroyed Phillip's life, I sought out some new guys who had just come in. One of those was Gary Hasha, who was already an alcoholic, so it was easy to persuade him to use drugs with us. I cannot remember a day that Gary did not stumble into our room drunk or high.

Another problem soldier with a bad attitude arrived in our barracks late one night and immediately went out and got drunk. When he returned from his partying, he started hollering, cursing, and disturbing everyone. He stumbled over to our card game and began to let all of us know that he was not scared of anybody. I told him to shut up and go get a shower.

He screamed, "You can't tell me what to do. I'll whip you all over this room."

I climbed over the card table and told him once again to shut up. He then ripped his shirt off and yelled, "I'm Ronald Orr. I'm from Stockton, Calif...."

I hit him right between the eyes and as he went down, I leaned over him saying, "I'm Danny Aber. I'm from El Campo, Texas. Glad to meet you. Now go get that shower."

A few nights later, Ron got into another fight with a guy named Mike Epson. Rick and I had to pull Mike off of Ron after he almost cut his ear off with a broken beer bottle. It took about ten stitches to put Ron's ear back on.

After that happened, I began to feel sorry for Ron. One night I took him to a disco in Frieburg. We were both high on hash and he began to act a little crazy, so I left him there. The next day we were told that Ron had been beaten up and left on the side of the road. When he was taken to the 97th General Hospital, he was acting strange so the doctors put him in the psychiatric ward for observation.

After his release, he was never quite the same. He didn't have much to say to anyone and soon became a loner. I felt guilty about what had happened and made sure I always gave him some dope when it came in, or took him to a bar occasionally for a few drinks.

Things continually worsened until our room was totally out of control. We were all living on borrowed time, every one of us. All of this may seem hard to believe, but unfortunately it is the truth. Had it not been for Rick Blommer, things would have been worse. He was the sensible one, the peacemaker. He was the only one who could reason with me and some of the other guys. In spite of all his efforts, things would still get worse.

In June of 1979, a carnival came to town and we all headed that way. When we arrived we were stoned, as usual, and acting crazy. I decided to get on a ride. The idea was to rock a cage using your own weight until you got the cage spinning in a circle. As I began to rock the cage, it got faster and faster until I started getting dizzy. All of a sudden, I heard a loud pop and immediately I thought a board must have fallen out of the floor of the cage. I found myself on my back looking up and being thrown from one side of the cage to the other. I began to feel an awful pain in my leg, and screamed for help. When the cage finally stopped rocking, my friends pulled me out and called the dispensary. My knee began to swell immediately and the pain was almost unbearable. Worried about being stoned when they took me to the dispensary, I told the driver to take me to my room, but the sergeant in charge insisted I see the doctor.

When I arrived at the dispensary, the doctor was immediately aware of my drug use, and began to counsel me. I was afraid he would report me, but again nothing was said.

After the examination, they informed me they would be sending me to the 97th General Hospital in Frankfurt. My knee had snapped in two while I was on the ride and there needed to be more tests and possibly emergency surgery.

During my third day at the 97th General Hospital, a young 17-year-old girl came into the room filling water pitchers. She quietly asked me if I got high. I told her, "Of course, doesn't everyone?"

She smiled and said, "I'll see you at six o'clock with some good hash."

At six o'clock sharp she was pushing me in a wheelchair to a veranda overlooking the emergency airlift area. We sat there for about two hours getting stoned and talking about how much we hated the Army. She told me her father was a doctor at the hospital and that she would stop in to see me everyday. We became good friends, and for the rest of my stay at the 97th, she supplied me with speed and hash.

Upon my release from the hospital, I was informed that I was still under doctor's care. Everyday I had to take a bus from Frieburg to the hospital for therapy.

During this time, I was my own boss and did not have to answer to anyone. The doctor gave me a "permanent profile," which exempted me from any type of duty. For the next six months I never put on another uniform, or stood in another formation. I came and went whenever I wanted, partied all night, and stayed away from the concern as much as possible.

I began to grow more and more bitter, hating everyone. I was doing more speed and would stay up for three days at a time until I would pass out, and then sleep for two days straight.

I began to do some cocaine and at one point I even tried heroin. I was looking for something, but for what, I had no idea. I was getting more and more violent; I was cursing, throwing and breaking things.

One of my sergeants came in the room one day and announced he was putting a new boy over me and that I was going to have to double bunk.

"No!" I angrily protested.

"I outrank you, Aber, and what I say goes," he declared.

Taking the walking cane I'd been using, I broke it over the corner of my bed, put it to his throat, and defiantly protested, "No! I said."

I looked over at Phillip and told him, "The new boy stays above you."

Phillip reluctantly agreed, "That's fine with me."

Looking back to Sergeant Bell, I removed the broken cane from his throat and said, "There, everything is settled."

I don't know why Bell did not call the Military Police right then. He could have had me locked up for a long time and been free of my threats. Instead, he just looked at me and yelled, "Aber, you're crazy. I'll be glad when they get rid of you!"

My life was on a steady decline after that episode. I was lawless. I started black marketing cigarettes and liquor, making between $800-$1,500 a month.

In the month of September, I was busted for having rationed items in a German's car. I was very lucky because I did not have any cigarettes or liquor on me that day. I tried to con my way out of that situation, but I knew the Military Police did not really believe me, especially after examining my ration card. All they did was take my name, my company's name, and the name of my company commander.

After that close call, I decided to stay away from black marketing as much as possible. I knew that I would be questioned about it soon.

The month of October brought about many changes at the concern, because of six young men. They bought some heroin that was laced with poison and all six of them died the same day. Because of the severity of this problem, General Haig had everyone on the parade field standing at attention.

I was over at the dispensary watching as groups of soldiers were taken in for urinalysis tests. Things got real tight from that day on. There were drug searches at two and three o'clock in the morning, with dogs and Military Police three times a week. Uncle Sam was out to get anyone who was a user now. They were determined to rid the Army of these unwanted elements. Because of my drug addiction, I began to stay away from the concern as much as possible.

While I was moving around, partying and making contacts to sell some cigarettes and liquor, I made a sell to a German man from a small community for about $900. I also bought some dope (hashish), so I decided to take all the guys to the pizza place up the road and party. I had the drugs, the money, and the respect of all those guys. I was the life of the party. After about an hour of hard drinking, a soldier came in looking for Danny Aber. I was standing on top of a table telling jokes; I climbed down and asked him what it was about. He told me he was just the C.Q.'s runner, but that TOP wanted to see me right away. It seemed important.

I was really scared now because I assumed it was about the time I was questioned in Frankfurt for black marketing.

As I walked up the hill to TOP's office I was thinking of a good explanation to give him for what happened that day in Frankfurt.

I could see something was bothering TOP as I entered his office. He was not in a good mood.

I laughed, and asked, "What's up, TOP? I got here as fast as I could. I was up the street with the guys having a party!"

He then asked me if I had received any phone calls from Texas. I assured him I had not, and then he looked straight into my glassy eyes and pronounced, "Aber, your father passed away today. Your father died."

I was stunned. I could not believe it. Puzzled, I questioned, "My father? He's only forty-six. Was it an accident or what?"

Lowering his eyes to the floor, he softly said, "No, it was a heart attack."

Standing right there I began to cry. The only stabilizing factor in my life was now gone. The very reason I was in the Army was to prove to my dad that I could be good at something.

As I turned away, TOP assured me they would be working on getting me home for the funeral as soon as possible. He asked me where I would be going in case they needed me. I told him I would be in my room.

TOP's reply was ever so clear. With a look of sympathy, he commented, "I guess

the party's over."

2

You Gotta Serve Somebody

Two days after I received the news of my father's death, I was on my way to the States for the funeral. I was so bitter by now, I hated everything and everyone. I blamed the Army, my mother, and the rest of my family for what I was feeling. I was very upset because I was the only one in my family who did not have a chance to see my father before he died. All of the drugs, money, and popularity I had acquired could not erase the pain I was feeling. I wanted to see my dad, to talk to him, to tell him that I was sorry, or just to say thank you. There were things that needed to be said, but now the opportunity was gone and I had to live with the consequences. The guilt was almost too great to bear. I guess I was looking for forgiveness from the most important person in my life, but it was too late.

By the day of the funeral, the bitterness and hatred had mounted so much that I was blaming my mother for the events that had transpired in my life. The situation was so bad that after the service, my oldest brother, Rickey, and I almost had a fight. Messed up and depressed, I grabbed what little clothes I had and left. I ended up at the house of an old high school friend, Lawrence Roy. We partied and smoked dope for the next three weeks. I was getting worse than ever, but I just did not care anymore.

By now I was so full of bitterness that I did not even like myself. I did not speak to my mother one time during those three weeks, and while I was on my way to the airport heading back to Germany, I stopped by to tell her I was leaving. I knew she needed me, but all I could do was say good-bye.

Upon my return to Frankfurt, I found myself in an extreme dilemma. I wanted out of the Army and I wanted to get out right then. I talked to my commander and explained to him that I really needed to be with my mother, and that my little brother and sister were still at home and my mom needed help. We also talked about my future in the military. I explained how I felt my career in the military was over because of my knee injury.

"Sir, I'm not the kind of guy who can sit behind a desk," I insisted. I even had tears rolling down my face for added sincerity. Of course, the tears were not real and I lied about wanting to help my mom and the rest of the family. I was just looking for a way out of the Army as soon as possible. My story must have worked, because the commander told me that he would start the paperwork right away. However, he informed me that the possibilities of my getting out of the Army on a hardship discharge were very slim. One reason was that there was an older brother who was able to help my mother, and another reason was that Iran had just captured our embassy and we were on combat alert.

The Third Armour Division was on line to be in the first deployment to Iran. I would not be going because I was still under a doctor's care, but some of my friends were supposed to go, and that sobered them up quickly. They spent hours at the motor pool painting their tanks for desert combat. For almost a month nobody was allowed to leave the concern. The situation ended up being nothing more than "a sit and wait game." That was the only time I can remember when anyone of us in the military was glad Jimmy Carter was president.

As November passed, I continued to become very depressed. I was doing more drugs and drinking everyday, something I had never done before. I became a loner and very seldom spoke to anyone, except Rick. I even moved out of the fourth floor room to one on the third floor.

I do not know how to explain it, but there was a horrible spirit of oppression and suicide in Germany. I was not a Christian, or even religious at that time, but I could tell it was there. I could feel it every day, and even worse, I could see the hopelessness in everyone's eyes. I was contemplating suicide once again. Feeling as if I had reached the point of no return, drugged out, drunk, and full of bitterness, I could see no way out.

As I walked around the concern, I felt a heaviness come over me. It was telling me, "End it now! What are you waiting for? Your father's dead, and nobody cares about you. It would be better for everyone if you just end it now. Come on, do it; do it now!"

As I was passing the chaplain's office, something told me to go in. I walked through the doors, saw the receptionist, and respectfully asked her to please call a minister. She then informed me that all the Protestant ministers were out, but there was a priest available.

Two minutes later, I was sitting in the priest's office crying and pouring my heart out to him. I explained about the death of my father and my thoughts of committing suicide. I actually thought I was having a nervous breakdown, but when I was finished, all he did was lean over and pat me on the shoulder and say, "Young man, don't worry about those things, everybody goes through difficulties. It will work itself out; just have faith."

As I left his office, I felt that same heaviness come over me. It was as if a voice was telling me, "I told you nobody cared; you just wasted your time. There's only one way out. DO IT NOW! What's there to live for anyway?" When I reached the barracks, I went to Rick Blommer's room on the fourth floor, opened the windows, and stood in the opening getting ready to jump. As I looked down, I started to cry. I felt something pull me out of the window, as if someone was there with me. I sat on Rick's bed crying uncontrollably wondering what had just happened. It was then that I asked God to get me out of Germany and if He did I would do anything He said.

The very next day a sergeant from the headquarters office saw me and said, "Aber, you'll be home for Christmas. Your hardship discharge is final. You'll be leaving in one week." Needless to say, I was beside myself. I was getting out; I was going home.

Two nights before my departure, Rick decided to throw me a party. There was plenty of music, dope, and beer. Everyone was there to wish me good luck. Everything was going fine until Phillip walked in.

Phillip had straightened his life back up and was playing G.I. Joe again. He was bragging about the coffee mug he had received for finishing in the top ten at a Non-Commissioned Officer School. It was a great accomplishment and worthy of notice, but not at my party. While he was talking, he set his coffee mug on the card table right beside me. When I saw it, I became bitter. I could have won it. After all, I was a better soldier, but here I was sitting around a table stoned and drunk, a loser. I shoved the coffee mug off the table onto the floor. As it hit the floor the handle broke. The room became quiet and everybody was staring at the broken coffee mug. Phillip drew back and hit me right in back of the head. I was surprised because he had never done that before, but I guess he was fed up with my antics.

I turned and pushed him into Rick's wall locker. I hit him as hard and fast as I could, hating everything he stood for. I bursted his bottom lip and blackened his eye, and probably would have hurt him more had Rick not pulled me off him.

The next day was total chaos. My Platoon Sergeant, Elliot, was trying to get Phillip to press charges against me. Elliot wanted me to go to jail, not home. But Phillip refused; he let me walk free. I was going home.

I left Germany on December 23, 1979. I was uncertain of what the future was holding for me. On the plane back to the

States, I sat beside a young man whose wife was picking him up after we processed out. He asked me if I needed a ride to the airport and informed me that he had some good dope waiting. I quickly accepted his offer.

I was stoned when I reached the Delta counter. After fumbling to find my ticket for a few minutes, I apologized to the lady and boarded the plane for Houston.

Once in Houston, I caught a bus to El Campo. I reached my mom's house about 7:30 the morning of the 24th. As she answered the door she was shocked because she did not know that I was coming home. We talked for a little while, and then I called my friend Lawrence in Edna, Texas. That night I moved in with him and it was party time again.

I went to work for the same company my father had worked for just before he died. I smoked pot nonstop. I would wake up in the morning and smoke a joint, have another one on the way to work, one during my lunch break, and have a few on the way home.

Every day I would sit and get wasted, then Lawrence and I would head to the bars. We would stay out until two or three o'clock in the morning, wake up at five o'clock, ready for work. It was a miracle that we were not killed in an accident. We ended up in a ditch many times. I was lawless; I did not care about anything or anyone. I was a user. As long as someone had something to give me, I would use them. When their usefulness was no longer a factor, I would find someone else.

I was staying stoned and even using speed on a daily basis just to keep going. I also started skipping work regularly, but I always had an excuse for my actions. I was wearing thin on Lawrence because my actions were so erratic. My lack of concern for my job and my pathetic lazy ways of sitting around drinking and getting stoned really bothered him.

I was sitting around the house smoking pot, getting ready to go party one night, when I received a call from Mobil Oil Production, the second largest oil company in the world. They told me they wanted me to come and work for them.

Needless to say, I was shocked. I told them, "Sure, as soon as possible."

But there was one stipulation. I would have to move to Bay City, Texas, about 45 miles away. That may not sound like much of a move, but I had many bad memories of Bay City and I was not sure I was ready to face them yet. This was the reason I had been running for the last four years. I thought for a minute, and assured them that the move was all right with me. I just could not pass up an opportunity like that one.

My first day on the job was very different. My coworkers were three older men who were all about one or two years away from retirement. We did not break any speed records. We rode around in a truck and gauged a few wells, stopped at the Baptist church for donuts, returned to the office to do some paperwork, and then we would go home. I had a feeling I was going to really enjoy this job.

After ten days on the job, I moved from Edna, Texas, to Bay City. Ben, who was a friend of my older brother, allowed me to stay at his trailer house. Even though Ben was a quiet person, a bit more private than myself, we still partied. Almost every day we would sit and smoke a few joints and play backgammon. I do not think I ever beat him, but we always had fun playing.

Ben had his other friends, so I mostly went back to El Campo to party with Lawrence and another friend named Mike.

We were planning a party for April 5, 1980. It was a Saturday night and Mike's parents would be going out of town and their huge two-story house would be all ours.

There was plenty of pot and beer for everyone that night. As we were getting things ready for the party, my friend and I went upstairs and did some cocaine and then got crazy and baked some marijuana brownies. By the time the party started, we were wasted. The house was packed with people and the music was blaring. AC/DC was singing, "I'm on a highway to hell." Van Halen shouted from the vinyl record, "Running with the devil."

I had eaten five marijuana brownies, smoked about six joints, snorted two rails of cocaine, and was on about my seventh glass of beer when I felt as if my heart stopped. I was sitting at the table ready to play some poker and my head went down and hit the table. I could hear and see, but I could not move. Mike and Lawrence had to help me to the living room. I do not know when, but shortly after that, I passed out. I do remember people slapping me in the face, but I was unable to respond. Eventually, I ended up in the master bedroom. How I got there I still do not know. I woke up about seven the next morning and walked downstairs. I heard this song by Bob Dylan playing and it really irritated me. He whined in his unique style:

> "God don't make promises that He don't keep;
> You got some big dreams baby, but in order to dream you got to still be asleep;
> When are you going to wake up, When are you going to wake up,
> When are you going to wake up and strengthen the things that remain?
> Do you ever wonder just what God requires?
> You think that He's just an errand boy to satisfy your wandering desires;
> When are you going to wake up, When are you going to wake up,
> When are you going to wake up and strengthen the things that remain?"

I know this might sound funny, but at that moment I remembered the promise I had made God when He pulled me out of that window in Germany. I shook it off and headed to the kitchen for a beer and a joint. But that song kept echoing in my head, "When you gonna wake up, when you gonna wake up?"

As I turned to go to the living room, I saw Mike and his girlfriend on the back patio, smoking a joint. I went and took the joint from him and took a big drag. As I was about to turn away, Mike looked at me and said, "Aber, I was worried about you last night. You know what you need?"

"No, what?" was my reply.

He smiled and took a drag off the joint and said, "You need God, the Holy Spirit, you need to go to church."

I then quickly asked him, "If that's what I need how come it ain't helping you? And who are you to sit there with your girlfriend smoking dope and drinking beer trying to tell me what I need? I sure don't need your kind of religion or church, Mike."

Turning to leave, I passed the stereo and heard the same record playing. I noticed there were album covers scattered all over the floor. All except for one. It was leaning against the fireplace all by itself. It had a picture of a man looking up at a cross. Picking up the album, tears filled my eyes. I realized at that moment I had to make good on that promise I made to God in Germany. As I turned the album cover over, I noticed that someone had written in big bold letters:

"YOU GOTTA SERVE SOMEBODY.

It may be the devil or it may be the LORD, but you're gonna have to serve somebody."

3

Radical Adjustments to Extreme Dilemmas

I left Mike's house and headed for Bay City. When I reached the house, Ben was smoking a joint and listening to some Eddie Rabbit. He asked me if I wanted to play a game of backgammon. I agreed and rolled a joint. While Ben was setting up the board, I could not stop thinking about Mike's comments to me earlier that day. I knew he was right; I did need to get my life together.

During the game, a young man named Greg Barnes popped into my head. He was a converted surfer and drug user who had witnessed to me about four years earlier.

I asked Ben if he remembered Greg, and Ben replied sarcastically, "Yeah, I know him. He's still a Jesus freak."

I knew right then that I needed to see Greg. He must have found something real if he was still serving God after four years. I went to bed that night planning to contact Greg the next day.

The next morning I went to work with that crazy song still stuck in my mind, "When you gonna wake up, when you gonna wake up," and I could see the album cover with the words "You Gotta Serve Somebody," written across the front.

The next day the men I worked with asked me if anything was wrong, because I was not talking very much. My foreman was a Baptist deacon and I thought about talking to him, but he smoked almost three packs of cigarettes a day and every once in a while a curse word would slip out, so I decided to wait until I looked up Greg Barnes.

After work, I drove to Greg's house and knocked on the door. His sister answered and said that he was not home from work yet, so I decided to go and get something to eat. After two hours I went back and was told he had just stepped out and would be home later. I had some time to waste, so I drove over to the Dairy Queen where most of the kids hung out. Some girls I used to party with saw me and one named Becky hollered, "Come on, Danny. Let's go get high."

I climbed into her car, and as we started to leave the parking lot, a voice said, "Get out of the car, NOW, Greg is home."

I did not know where the voice came from, but it seemed so real that I had to acknowledge it. I shouted, "Becky, stop the car NOW! I'm sorry, but I have to go somewhere else."

They were all looking at me as if I were crazy, but I knew I had to listen to the voice. As I crawled out of the car, I felt that this was probably the last time God would have dealt with me.

I left the Dairy Queen feeling something I had never felt before. I was crying when I reached Greg's house. I did not know anything about God or the Bible, but I knew what I was doing was the right thing. I knocked on the door and Greg answered. He still had that big smile and a glow on his face. He looked at me and asked, "Danny, is that you?"

I put my head on his shoulder and began crying and saying, "Greg, help me. I can't live like this anymore."

Greg put his arm around my shoulder and told me to repent.

On his doorstep, I began to pour out my heart to God, emptying myself of everything. When I had finally died out to self, God took away all the bitterness, anger, and hatred I had accumulated the past six years. I had repented, and I was forgiven.

Greg invited me into his house, and we had a Bible study on baptism and receiving the Holy Ghost. I had a great time and I felt happier than ever before. Greg invited me to hear the New Life Quartet on Wednesday night. I told him I would be there.

The next two days were really strange. I did not talk to anyone about my repenting and my decision to be baptized. No one at my job had ever spoken about religion or church, but the day after I repented, my boss told me he had put my name down as his guest to a potluck dinner on Wednesday night, the night I was supposed to be baptized. I accepted his invitation. After all, he was my boss.

On Wednesday morning, I remembered I was to be baptized at Greg's church, and my boss reminded me of the potluck dinner at the Baptist church. Knowing that I needed to be baptized, I went to see the Baptist pastor after work. His secretary informed me he was unavailable.

I said, "You don't understand. I need to talk to him right now."

She told me, "He's not seeing anyone today."

"But you don't understand. I need to be baptized right now or tonight," I insisted.

Laughing, she said, "It doesn't matter anyway, we only baptize on the last Sunday of the month. Sorry."

I looked at her and thought to myself, "Well, you can keep your potluck dinner, too."

As I was leaving, I noticed the Methodist church right across the street. I was raised Methodist, so I walked in expecting to receive a warm greeting.

When the secretary spotted me, she rudely inquired, "What do you want?"

"Nothing." I replied. I turned and walked out. I realized that that definitely was not the friendliest church in town.

After two close encounters of the third kind, I decided to go and see my old scout master. After three hours of visiting,

I realized it was too late to go to church, so I went home. As I pulled the front door open, I saw Ben and a friend sitting on the couch smoking a joint. Right then I realized how ugly sin really was.

Ben excitedly informed me, "Steppin' Out is playing at the Silver Dollar. Get cleaned up and let's go."

I quickly replied, "No, not tonight. I'm going to church."

That must have been a shocker for them, because I never turned down an opportunity to go dancing. It was already 8:30 p.m.; I would be late, but I would still go. I cleaned up and put on a gold chain with a big #1 on it (I thought a lot of myself back then). I went straight to the church. As I sat in my truck in the church parking lot, I put my head on the steering wheel and prayed, "God, if You're real and this church is real, let me know it tonight."

When I opened the door to the church, I felt as if something cut me in half and everything that was bad about me fell off. It was right there I realized that Jesus was God. I stepped through the double doors into the back of the church and saw teenagers, young married couples, and the older folks lifting their hands worshiping God together. I was so impressed. One of the singers in the quartet, who had not seen me walk in, stopped singing and said, "I feel like God just touched someone tonight."

I ran to the altar and began to thank God for touching me. Pastor M.J. Moore walked over and laid his hand on my head and I immediately began to speak in other tongues. He baptized me in the name of Jesus.

I was so excited and on fire that I could not believe what was happening to me. I had never felt this way before in my life. I was not only higher than any drug had ever made me, but now I felt clean and lighter than normal. There was a heavy load that was lifted from me that night. All the hatred and bitterness was gone. I finally found Danny Aber, when I found God.

Society will scream about everyone's rights. It will tell you to experiment with life, the sky is the limit, do whatever feels good. Do not let anyone tell you what to do. Do not listen to your parents, teachers, your pastor or the Bible, just go and find out for yourself. What people fail to realize is that we are made in the image of God, and if you want to find yourself, you have to first find God.

I will never forget April 9, 1980, as long as I live. It was the new start for which I had always been looking. After service, I went home and started packing my bags. Ben asked me what I was doing. I told him, "I went to the Pentecostal church. I got the Holy Ghost, and was baptized in Jesus' name. I don't live here anymore!"

Ben laughed and assured me it was not going to last.

I responded, "I don't know how long it will last, but I still don't live here."

I grabbed what few clothes I had and went to the Bay-Tex Hotel. I drove those drunks crazy that night witnessing to everyone about what had happened to me just a few hours earlier.

I woke up the next morning, called the office and told them I had some personal business I needed to attend to. I got a haircut and then drove to El Campo, to Young's Grocery Store. I walked into the store, and feeling the power of God, I asked to see Mr. Young. When he came to the counter I asked, "Do you remember me?"

He looked at me and squinted his eyes for a few seconds replying, "Yeah, you used to come in here about three or four years ago, right?"

I quickly responded, "Yes, Sir, I used to come and steal things. But last night I went to the First Pentecostal Church in Bay City, and I received the Holy Ghost and was baptized in Jesus' name. I've come to pay you off!"

Placing some money on the counter in front of him, I said, "This should be more than enough to cover what I stole."

Tears began to roll down his face as he put his big hands over the money and pushed it back toward me, saying, "I don't want this."

But I insisted that he take it. I told him, "I am making restitution."

I went to everyone I could remember selling drugs to or partying with and knocked on their doors. As they opened them, they would see me standing there smiling, telling them, "I came to apologize. I want you to forgive me for selling you dope or anything else I did against you. You see, I went to the First Pentecostal Church in Bay City last night and I received the Holy Ghost and was baptized in Jesus' name. I want you to know that Jesus loves you."

Many of them were too shocked to say anything and the rest probably did not believe me at that moment. Nevertheless, I did what I felt I needed to do to make things right. Nobody told me I had to do those things, but I believed it was necessary for me to be saved. Believe me, my conversion was the talk around all my old hangouts.

I saw God do great miracles in my life. Not one time was I ever tempted to drink, smoke dope, or curse from April 9, 1980, on. I was serving a merciful God who kept His hand on me through all of the broken promises I had made Him; He was faithful.

One of my favorite songs says, "He healed my body, He touched my mind, He saved me just in time."

On April 9, 1980, God made a

radical adjustment to my extreme dilemma.

4

Aber's God Is Tough!

hree weeks into my conversion, I was running full throttle. No sinner was safe in Bay City now. I was wrapped up, tied up, and tangled all up in Jesus.

I moved into a trailer house with two young men from the church. We would sit for hours studying the Word of God, and marking all the Scriptures on baptism and the One God. I made it a point to go to the church and pray everyday and afterward I would go out to witness.

One Saturday morning about three weeks after I had moved out of Ben's house, I was trying to catch somebody I wanted to witness to. I ended up on Horn Road close to Ben's trailer house, so I decided to go talk to him. When he answered the door, I could tell he was upset, so I asked him what was wrong.

He said, "My sister Marcy is in the hospital in Victoria, and it don't look like she is going to live. Mom went up today."

I quickly replied, "Ben, God is real. He can help her."

Ben shot back, "I don't want to hear about your God, Aber." He swung the front door open, pointed to the sky and said, "If your God is real, why is my sister dying, why is this happening?"

I assured him that if his sister was sincere, God would heal her today. I had no idea where that answer came from because I did not even know one Scripture that dealt with healing. I had heard Pastor Moore say, "God still heals and He wants to heal you tonight." So I just parroted what I heard my pastor say.

Ben looked at me and said, "Maybe you believe that, but I don't. Now get out of my way, I'm going to play golf." He grabbed his golf bag and stepped out the door. I climbed into my truck and headed for Victoria; I was going to pray for Marcy.

I drove the 75 miles to Victoria and was so pumped up and full of belief that God was going to heal her that I spoke in tongues most of the way there. I arrived at the hospital and headed for the information desk. A few moments later I was standing at her door. I asked God to save her, reminding Him that He was not willing that any should perish.

I knocked on her door and a nurse answered, "What do you need?"

I replied, "I want to see Marcy."

"You can't, young man, she is not doing well and only the family members are allowed in," she insisted.

"But you don't understand. I'm from the First Pentecostal Church and I came to pray for Marcy," I urged.

I then heard Mrs. Manry ask, "Who is it?"

I answered, "It's Danny; I used to live with your son, Ben. I go to the First Pentecostal Church in Bay City. I've come to pray for Marcy."

She told the nurse to let me in. I was not ready for what I saw when I entered. Marcy was laying there frail, and as white as the sheets on her bed. She was as close to death as I had ever seen anyone. The doctors had given her up and I felt that she had given up also.

I had not yet learned about anointing with oil and I had never seen anyone healed. After all, I was just three weeks old in the Lord. So I just sat down beside her on the bed with my new Thompson Chain Bible with gold trim, and told her, "Marcy, I don't know if you can hear me, but it's not God's will for anyone to die lost. Now, if God is going to save you, He is going to have to heal you first. If you want to be saved, God will heal you right now."

The only Scriptures in the Bible I knew were salvation Scriptures. I started with *John 3:3 and 5,* which says, "Jesus answered and said unto him, Verily, verily, I say unto thee, Except a man be born again, he cannot see the kingdom of God. Jesus answered, Verily, verily, I say unto thee, Except a man be born of water and of the Spirit, *he cannot enter into the kingdom of God.*"

And then I read her *Acts 2:38,* "Then Peter said unto them, Repent, and be baptized *every one of you* in the name of Jesus Christ *for the remission of sins,* and *ye shall receive* the gift of the Holy Ghost."

I next turned to *Acts 8:14-17,* "Now when the apostles which were at Jerusalem heard that Samaria *had received the word of God,* they sent unto them Peter and John: Who, when they were come down, prayed for them, that they might receive the Holy Ghost: (For as yet he was fallen upon none of them: only they were baptized in the name of the Lord Jesus.) Then laid they their hands on them, and they received the Holy Ghost."

I then turned to *Acts 10:44-48,* "While Peter yet spake these words, the Holy Ghost *fell on all them which heard the word.* And they of the circumcision which believed were astonished, as many as came with Peter, *because that on the Gentiles also* was poured out the gift of the Holy Ghost. *For they heard them speak with tongues, and magnify God.* Then answered Peter, Can any man forbid water, *that these should not be baptized,* which have received the Holy Ghost as well as we? And he commanded them to be baptized in the name of the Lord. Then prayed they him to tarry certain days."

I moved quickly to *Acts 19:1-5,* "And it came to pass, that, while Apollos was at Corinth, Paul having passed through the upper coasts came to Ephesus: and *finding certain disciples*, He said unto them, Have ye received the Holy Ghost since ye believed? And they said unto him, *We have not so much as heard whether there be any Holy Ghost.* And he said unto them, Unto what then were ye baptized? And they said, *Unto John's baptism.* Then said Paul, John verily baptized with the baptism of repentance, saying unto the people, that they should believe on him which should come after him, that is, on Christ Jesus. *When they heard this*, they were baptized in the name of the Lord Jesus."

I explained to her how they had already been baptized, but they needed the name of Jesus attached to their baptism.

I then went to my last Scripture, *Acts 22:16*, "*And now why tarriest thou?* arise, and be baptised, and *wash away thy sins*, calling on the name of the Lord."

As soon as I finished reading that Scripture, the power of the Holy Ghost flooded the room. Marcy sat straight up in the bed and the color came back into her face.

Her mom began to cry. She was standing in the corner rubbing her arms with both of her hands, sobbing, "I don't believe it! I don't believe it!"

It was an instant miracle! Nurses began to run in and out of the room, while other patients who knew Marcy came in to see what was going on.

She sat up, and swinging her legs over the edge of the bed, declared, "I am going home."

One worried nurse immediately called the doctor. The other nurses stood there amazed as I was standing in the corner speaking in tongues while her mom was crying, rubbing her arms up and down as she was feeling the Holy Ghost. They were trying to figure out which of us needed help the most, Marcy, her mom or me.

About 30 minutes later the doctor came rushing into the room, pushed Marcy back on the bed, and placed the blood pressure cuff on her arm. It went, chooo, chooo, chooo, chooo and then let off, shhhhhhh. He shook his head a little and did it again. Again it went chooo, chooo, chooo, chooo and let off again shhhhhhh. He shook his head one more time as if he did not believe what was happening. He tightened it one more time, and pumped it slowly to make sure the read was accurate. Chooooo, chooooo, chooooo, chooooo and letting off again shhhhhhhhh, it sounded for the third time. He turned and looked at Marcy and said, "I don't know what happened, but everything is fine. Your blood pressure is normal."

Marcy quickly responded, "I'm going home."

The doctor, obviously worried, pleaded with her to stay just a few more days. He said he would not recommend that she leave yet, but Marcy insisted.

She left the hospital that afternoon walking under her own power, or should I say God's power? After we reached her mother's house, she sat in the living room drinking a soda and eating soup when Ben walked in carrying his golf bag. Not knowing Marcy was there, he called out to his mother asking, "How is Marcy doing?"

When he turned toward the living room he saw Marcy sitting there, just about six hours after his conversation with me. Dropping his golf bag, Ben stood there shaking his head saying,

"Aber's God is tough!"

5

The Consequences of Divine Exposure

The next morning, Marcy was in church with her mother and Mrs. Galley, a good friend of the family. Mrs. Galley was from the Catholic church and voiced her opinion of Pentecost. "I don't believe people really speak in tongues." But she could not deny the miracle that had happened to Marcy.

After the preaching that morning, Marcy went straight to the altar and began to repent. Mrs. Galley was right beside her watching in amazement. About five minutes later, Marcy was filled with the Holy Ghost and fell into Mrs. Galley's arms and spoke in tongues for at least 30 minutes. Needless to say, Mrs. Galley retracted her statement about tongues after that service.

Something happened to me when Marcy was baptized in Jesus' name. I became addicted to soul winning. Receiving the Holy Ghost and being baptized in Jesus' name was great, but watching someone you brought to church receive the Holy Ghost and get baptized surpasses everything else.

That night, I received a burden for the people of Bay City. I went everywhere telling people about Jesus. While I was standing in front of the post office handing out tracts to everyone who passed by, Ben walked by me into the building and did not say a word. But as he was leaving, he stopped and said, "You really believe that stuff, don't you, Danny?"

I smiled and replied, "Yes, Ben, with all my heart." He continued on, but deep down I knew someday Ben would experience Pentecost for himself.

I bewildered many people during those few weeks. No one actually believed I would last, but they failed to realize I was now a new creature in Christ, and that all the old things had passed away, and all things had become new.

The men I worked with were not at all thrilled about my newfound joy. They tried their best to discourage me, but their attempts were in vain. When they would use a curse word, I would yell, "Praise the Lord" or "Hallelujah." They would just grumble and go their way, shaking their heads in dismay.

One day I was working with my boss, the Baptist deacon. We were tightening a valve on one of the oil wells when my pipe wrench slipped. I bursted my knuckles and they started to bleed. I grabbed my hand and said, "Thank You, Jesus!"

My boss went ballistic and started screaming, "Thank you, Jesus? Thank You, Jesus? Jesus can't help you. Why would you say 'Thank You, Jesus,' when you bursted your knuckles?"

Looking up at my boss, I replied, laughing, "Because Jesus is the only one who can help me. You're too busy screaming and hollering."

I could not remember laughing and just having fun before finding Jesus. There was a boldness that consumed me; I was not afraid to witness to anyone. I USED EVERY OPEN DOOR available TO ME. I even went to the police station and apologized to the policemen I had caused problems with. As I was giving my testimony, the police chief was listening intently. I noticed tears running down his face. I had no idea that he was a backslider.

I was just beginning to see the hand of God working in my life. I went to my pastor and told him I wanted to be the best soul winner in the church. Pastor Moore said with a smile, "Show me. Don't tell me."

I think the biggest impact my pastor had on my life was his burden for the lost. I remember when I was only a couple days old in the Lord, I walked into the church and saw Pastor Moore was on his face travailing for Bay City. I had never heard anything like that before in my life. Pastor Moore grew mightily in my eyes that day. He reminded me of Daniel, when he was praying and fasting for his people and his city, and God sent him skill and understanding. That is what happened in Bay City, Pastor Moore was a man of prayer and fasting and God gave him skill and understanding to see me and many others saved.

I asked Pastor Moore, "What can I do to win more souls?"

He smiled and said, "Go start a jail ministry."

I figured that was all right, no matter how badly I preached, they could not leave. Pastor drove me to the sheriff's department and let me give my testimony to the sheriff. After hearing my testimony, the sheriff gave me permission to preach every Sunday at the county jail.

My first Sunday was very rewarding. I walked into the dark, musty cell block, stepped over the stale bread and cigarette butts and went straight to the biggest cell.

There was a Baptist man and an Assembly of God man speaking to two or three people in separate corners of the big cell.

Not knowing any better, I figured they needed a little excitement. So I shouted, "PRAISE THE LORD EVERYBODY! LET'S HAVE CHURCH!" Needless to say, I had EVERYONE'S ATTENTION.

I began to give my testimony. I was talking about 100 mph with gusts up to 120 mph. As I was testifying, a big fat Mexican man reading a magazine kept looking over his shoulder at me. He then flung the magazine to the other side of the cell, got up and walked over to where I was standing. When I finished with my testimony, there were 12 men gathered close to the bars looking at the fat Mexican man closest to me who was now crying uncontrollably. Over to my left I saw two other young men crying also.

After I gave them an altar call, Lupe, the Mexican man, Doug, and Joe wanted to know more about what I was saying. Staying for an extra hour, I taught them about the One True God, repentance, baptism and the Holy Ghost.

I promised to pray for them at church that night, but Lupe interrupted, "We need more than prayers, we go to court Wednesday and all three of us have broken probation. In Texas, that will get you sent to the big house [prison]." As I was leaving, the other inmates were hassling them, laughing and then yelling, "All the praying in the world wouldn't keep you all out of prison."

That night I went to church fired up, telling everyone about the response I received. I even testified about the service and the fat Mexican man, Lupe. We had special prayer for them and God moved in a tremendous way. I went to the jail and visited them the following day. They were really discouraged. Their lawyers had just left and had not given them much hope of release.

I prayed with them through the bars of the cell. I was believing God for another miracle. Wednesday afternoon I received a phone call. It was Joe and Lupe, they were at the county jail, asking me to come and pick them up.

When I arrived, they were both smiling from ear to ear. They could not believe what had just taken place.

They told of how all the inmates were laughing before court saying, "You better hope God heard that preacher boy's prayers."

Joe was now telling me about his meeting with the judge. He said the judge looked up at him and back down at the paper with the charges and then back at him saying, "I don't know why I'm going to do this, but I am giving you another chance. But if I see you in this court again, I will have no mercy."

Joe excitedly said, "Danny, I was charged with breaking and entering a Texaco service station, which meant I broke my probation; I should be in prison. But God did it; God did it. He got me out."

Lupe had the same testimony. He also was released. I asked about the other young man named Doug. Joe replied, "He was released also, but since he was from Florida he had to go back. He's on a bus somewhere between here and Florida now."

That night Joe and Lupe were sitting in church about three rows from the back.

Pastor Moore taught on repentance that night and within ten minutes Joe was crying, repenting right there in his pew.

Lupe was playing the tough guy, but he soon gave in to the Holy Ghost as tears ran down his face.

After the teaching, Joe literally ran to the altar, repented and was baptized in Jesus' name. He received the Holy Ghost as he came out of the water. He experienced the consequences of divine exposure.

However, Lupe never repented. He just sat there crying, "I'm not ready. I'm just not ready."

I'm sorry to say, but about four months later Lupe was sent to prison for breaking his probation again. Had he yielded to the Holy Ghost, things could have been different. The sad thing was that he was so close to being set free.

Things were happening fast in the jail ministry. During my first year, 39 inmates received the Holy Ghost and many were baptized in Jesus' name.

During that time, I saw a murderer receive the Holy Ghost after he repented for about one-and-a-half hours. It was a tremendous witness to everyone in the cell.

It was about one month into my jail ministry that the Baptist and Assemblies of God ministers quit coming, so I had the jail to myself.

That was when I met Ted, who was in for being an accomplice to murder. As I was witnessing to him, I saw the hunger in his eyes. Usually everyone in jail says he is innocent. However, Ted never denied his involvement in the crime. This enabled him to realize his need for divine help.

I sat down in the stale bread and cigarette butts and taught him "Search for Truth" Bible study for almost four hours. He responded and repented of his sins right in his cell with everyone listening.

The next Sunday afternoon I taught him a Bible study on baptism and he immediately requested to be buried in the name of Jesus.

I went to church that night and told Pastor Moore of Ted's desire to be baptized.

The next morning we went to the sheriff and asked to baptize Ted. Sheriff Hurta assured us that Ted could not leave the jail facilities because he was in for murder. So Pastor Moore asked, "Sheriff, how are we going to baptize him? He does have a right to be baptized. And as you know, Sheriff, we immerse."

Hurta shook his head and rubbed his jaw and then after about 20 seconds of serious thinking, he answered, "I have a big bathtub in my office." He made the offer, certain we would decline.

Pastor Moore quickly accepted knowing Sheriff Hurta would have to be there, along with two of his deputies. So we were off to the office for the baptismal service. Pastor Moore baptized Ted in the wonderful name of Jesus. As he sat up in the bathtub, God filled him with the Holy Ghost. He spoke in tongues for at least 15 minutes while the sheriff and his deputies watched in amazement. They were eyewitnesses of Ted's transformation into a new creature.

I had about two months to teach Ted before his court date. We went through the "Search for Truth" Bible study. I saw a steady change in his life. He seemed to be maturing rapidly and was praying two or three hours a day. As his court date drew near, I noticed he maintained his faith in God. I was there in court when he received 15 years in the Texas Department of Correction. He leaned over and told the judge, "Thank you."

"Thank you?" questioned the judge, "Why thank me?"

Ted smiled and said, "Two months ago I repented of my sins and was baptized in Jesus' name and received the Holy Ghost. Your Honor, the next time you see me it will be on different terms."

The judge forced a smile, saying, "We'll see."

I had two more weeks with Ted before he was taken to prison. We laughed and studied the Word of God together waiting for his departure date.

When Ted left, he told me that he would write me as soon as he arrived at his permanent prison farm.

He was sent to the Ramsey One Unit and was made a trustee upon his arrival. This gave him more privileges than the others. He was able to listen to our Pentecostal preachers on the radio everyday. That was a tremendous blessing which helped establish him in God.

Ted spent over five years in the Texas Department of Correction. During that time I was able to have services every month at his unit. We would have at least 50 prisoners every service and many received the Holy Ghost and at least 20 were baptized.

I bought Ted a Thompson Chain Bible and sent him the *250 Home Bible Study Lessons.* He would sit up until one or two o'clock in the morning doing the lessons in his cell.

Ted was on fire and prison could not put him out. While at the Ramsey Unit he was given the last cell in the block because the guards knew they could trust him. The last cell was the farthest away from the guards and it was there the inmates would smoke their dope or do other illegal things.

One day as Ted was leaving his living quarters, a gang of four men approached him and demanded to use his cell to smoke some pot.

Without hesitation, Ted replied, "No, I don't think so. That cell has been dedicated to Jesus Christ and it won't be used for that."

They wanted to start trouble, but with the boldness Ted showed, they were not sure if they wanted to chance the embarrassment.

When Ted was about two months away from being released on good behavior, he was working at the tire shed and was approached by one of the bosses (guards). He was told to change some tires on his department vehicle, and he quickly obeyed. Three days later the same boss in the same truck entered Ted's shop and asked for four more new tires. Ted, standing there with a shocked look on his face, replied, "No."

That obviously irritated the boss so he walked up to Ted and yelled at him to change the tires. Ted reminded the guard about the four tires he had changed on Friday and refused to change them again. With about 25 other men looking on, the guard began to push Ted. He was yelling, "You're gonna lose your good time, boy. You're gonna have to fight me."

Ted did not give in to his demands. As the guard continued to provoke him, he took the harassment without saying a word; he just kept walking backward with every push. When Ted's back was against the wall of the shop, the guard started jamming him. Begging Ted to hit him, he said, "Just once I wish you would hit me, just once. You're gonna lose your good time, boy."

He then spit in Ted's face. As Ted looked around, all the men he had witnessed to were watching to see how he would react. Looking the guard straight in his eyes, Ted stressed, "Boss, five years ago I would have killed you, but that man died in a jail cell in Bay City, Texas, and was buried in a bathtub and arose to walk in newness of life. No, boss, I'm not going to fight you and I'm not going to change the tires either. It's illegal, and I can't do it."

For the next two months that man became one of Ted's friends. He allowed Ted to send gifts to people and have special visits because Ted had stood up for what was right.

When Ted was released from prison he stayed in our spare bedroom for a few weeks until he found a job. We had prayer meetings, Bible studies, and he even taught us to make the "Mexican Flag" hot sauce (tomatoes, onion, cilantro, and jalapeno pepper).

Upon his return to society, Ted received some excellent teaching at Tabernaculo De Vida, a Spanish church in Houston. The church reached out to Ted during his first month out of prison and helped him tremendously. He married a young woman from Pastor James Kilgore's church and now has two children.

The longer you're exposed to something, the more like that something you become. You walk differently, talk differently, and act differently, because you are exposed to the presence of God. We all need to experience

the consequences of divine exposure.

6

Thank You, Devil, Five Souls

bout one month into my walk with God, I had yet to experience anything except victory. I went from one mountaintop to the next. I was so fired up I would even shout when they sang "Amazing Grace."

This obviously bothered one of the elderly saints. She stopped me after a service one night and informed me, "Son, living for God isn't always a shout. You'll soon find out the devil is real."

Well, I just took what she said with a grain of salt. I did not let her words intimidate me, because I had never seen her shout. As a matter of fact, I had never even seen her smile.

While praying in the sanctuary one night about a week later, I could not feel anything. I tried to pray kneeling, standing, walking and even running around the church. I was so desperate that I even rolled on the floor, but all I felt was tired. My prayers seemed to hit the ceiling and come right back down. I had come down off of cloud nine and I hit hard. It was then I remembered what the woman had warned me about. At that moment I found out the devil was real. So I stood up and looked around and shouted, "Thank you, devil."

I knew that blew the devil's mind. Here I was, standing there, not able to feel anything and shouting, "Thank you, devil."

I then told the devil, "I can't see you, but I know you're here. And I just want to say, thank you. Thank you for reminding me you are real and because you reminded me you're real, I'm going to go and find five souls and witness to them right now."

I left the church and witnessed to five people I had never met before and three of the five came to church, received the Holy Ghost and were baptized in Jesus' name. All I could say was, "Thank you, devil, five souls."

After I received the Holy Ghost, I did not let a day go by that I did not ask God to give me the opportunity to find the men I was in the Army with. I wanted to ask their forgiveness and then tell them about the Gospel.

In 1981, I won Phillip Hooker to the Lord. He was in South Carolina when I tracked him down. I called him and apologized for what had happened in Germany. I invited him to Texas and assured him there were plenty of good jobs. He could not believe I could change in such a way, so he drove all the way to Texas, just to see if what I had was real.

His first Pentecostal service was a Friday night at Texas Camp Meeting. The Reverend R.E. Johnson was preaching, and it was a Holy Ghost blowout. Phillip saw over 5,000 Pentecostals worshiping and shouting, and others receiving the Holy Ghost. Because he did not know what was going on, Phillip left the service. After the service, I found him sitting on the hood of his car, smoking his Marlboro. Meeting my stare as I approached his car, Phillip shook his head and replied, "You guys are crazy."

"Why do you say that?" I asked.

He then boasted, "We don't act like that. I was born Baptist and I'll die Baptist."

Phillip stayed with my wife and me for about one month. He never made an effort to go to church.

On my way to a revival service one night, I had had enough of Phillip. He was sitting outside smoking a cigarette, so I approached him, offering him an ultimatum, "You be in the service tonight or find another place to live."

He argued, "I'm not going. That stuff is of the devil."

Well, when he said that, I pointed my finger in his face and reminded him of how I used to be and how I am now. Then I challenged him saying, "No, Phillip, we're not of the devil; you are. I'm not smoking or cursing; you are. You better check your religion." I then left for the revival service.

The service had just started, and we were standing worshiping God when I realized Phillip had walked in and had sat down by me. He leaned over and whispered, "You guys are crazy. I'll never jump around like that."

Of course, Phillip was right. When the Holy Ghost hit him, he did not jump, he rolled from one side of the church to the other.

It has been 14 years, and Phillip is still rolling for Jesus.

The next Army friend I pursued was Gary Hasha from California. I tracked him down and sent him a plane ticket to Houston. He received the Holy Ghost during his first service and was baptized in Jesus' name.

We spent many a night fishing under the lights at Matagorda, talking about how great God was and all of the blessings He had given us.

One night Gary broke down and cried while we were fishing. I asked him what was wrong, and he replied, "I'm just thankful you found me, Danny. I don't know what would have happened had you not cared enough to track me down and send me a plane ticket. I never really told you, but I love you. Thanks for everything."

Gary is still serving God in West Texas.

The third guy was my best friend in the Army, Rick Blommer. He also was from California. I located him in the summer of 1987. He was living in San Diego and had just gone through a divorce. He described his wife as a wonderful person, but she had a drug problem. He confessed, "Danny, we just couldn't work things out."

I knew he was distraught, so I told him I was sending him a plane ticket to come to Texas and visit me. He mumbled something about joining the Army again and was leaving in about ten days. I urged him to come if just for a day or two.

Two days later, he was in my home talking about Germany and telling my wife, Lori, how crazy I was. He could not believe the drastic change that had taken place in my life.

After showing Rick parts of Houston and Galveston, we went to Bay City so that he could see Phillip.

Rick stood there shaking his head, not believing that Phillip was serving God, also. Every time he looked at me he would just laugh, shake his head and remark, "I still don't believe it. Aber, a preacher; impossible."

That same night, Pastor Moore asked me to preach.

When I took the pulpit I knew of only one thing to do so I gave my testimony. As I was telling about what happened to me in Germany, Rick's head fell to his chest, tears ran down both sides of his face as he began to cry out to God. He repented right in the pew where he was sitting. While I was giving my testimony, I walked off the platform and stood in the very spot I had received the Holy Ghost seven years earlier. Turning and looking at Rick, I told him the Holy Ghost was for him also.

He ran to the altar and received the Holy Ghost in the very spot where God had given me the Holy Ghost. Rick was baptized in Jesus' name that night.

The next morning he was headed for San Diego full of the Holy Ghost. About a week later, he was in the Army again.

My family and I went to Costa Rica as AIMER's, but we kept in contact with him.

This brings me to the fourth man, Ronald Orr.

While we were on deputation headed west, we stopped in Amarillo, Texas. Our motor home broke down for the seemingly one hundredth time. I had it fixed and was about $500.00

in the hole already. We stopped and preached in Albuquerque, New Mexico, and were on the road again for Tucson, Arizona. We were driving a crippled motor home and limped into Flagstaff late one cold November night. I managed to pull the motor home into a parking lot by a JB's Restaurant before it died. It was cold and snowing and I was not in the best of moods. My son, Ryan, was watching me out of the window so I looked at him and raised my hand, and we hollered together, "Five souls, devil."

We spent the night in the parking lot and about six o'clock in the morning I cleaned up and went looking for my five souls. Entering the JB's Restaurant, I sat down beside a man and began to make conversation. He did not seem interested and left before his meal was finished. I next spoke with two waitresses, who were both very nice, but were working hard to keep up with their tables, so I did not receive any positive response out of either of them. The fourth was an Indian from the reservation and had definitely been drinking firewater, because he almost knocked me out when he breathed on me. I was zero for four and the devil was laughing it up. I was at the cashier area when the Holy Ghost started dealing with me not to leave, but I paid and walked out. As I turned to go back to the motor home, the Holy Ghost quickened me to look in the window. Sitting there by himself smoking a cigarette and drinking a cup of coffee was Ronald Orr, the fourth man I had been looking for for over 12 years. It was unbelievable. I immediately turned and walked back in and went straight to his table.

I leaned over the table and touched the young man on his shoulder, asking, "Is your name Ronald Orr?"

He looked up at me and nodded his head and then laid it on the table as tears began to flow. He raised his head and replied, "I have been sitting here all night and I was thinking about you, Aber, wondering where you were and what you were doing."

I then began to cry as I told him, "I'm a missionary to Panama, and I was praying I would see you to ask your forgiveness and tell you about what Jesus has done in my life."

Needless to say, when I knocked on the motor home door and introduced Ron to my family, Ryan was especially amazed. He could not believe God did it again for his dad.

Ron was an alcoholic, and was on the verge of a divorce. My wife and I went to Ron's apartment and met his wife, who was about to leave him. We shared with them what God did in our life and what God could do for them. Ron would start laughing and yell, "I don't believe it. You were worse than any of us. You were the one that started the parties."

I was so thankful God gave me that opportunity to see him. They followed us back to Bay City, Texas, and stayed through Christmas. Ron's wife was moved on in a service to be baptized in Jesus' name and she received the Holy Ghost. Ron was very repentant, but never made a move to be baptized or receive the Holy Ghost. I was glad that God gave me a chance to plant a seed in Ron's heart.

What were the chances of my finding Ron on deputation? I knew he was from California, and I was supposed to be in Tucson, but there I was sitting in Flagstaff, broken down next to where Ron was having breakfast.

I was so thankful. I raised my hand and shouted, "Five souls, devil."

Another exciting time came while on deputation. Everything seemed to be going wrong. My daughter, Leslie Victoria, had broken her arm in Augusta, Maine. We were now in Up-State New York, close to Syracuse and headed for Canada, when the air conditioner on top of the motor home blew off. As I pulled over and stopped by a field, I climbed up to examine the damage. It just needed to be screwed back down, but all I had was a cheap crescent wrench. If you know anything about tools, you would never own a cheap one. Well, I began to screw the air conditioner down, setting the wrench and then pulling. As the pressure was applied to the wrench, it separated and I busted my knuckles. I immediately shouted, "Thank you, devil, five souls. When I get to Canada, devil, I'm finding five souls."

Upon our arrival, we went right to the park where the youth crusade was taking place. Reverend R.E. Libby from Maryland was preaching. Everyone there seemed to be Pentecostal. But determined to find my five souls, I began to walk around asking God for a hungry soul. As I approached the concession stand, I saw a young boy with long hair sitting, writing on a sheet of paper (an application). I sat down beside him and introduced myself explaining why I was in Canada. He told me his name and I asked if he had ever heard of Pentecost. He replied, "No."

I then gave my testimony to Stephen. As he sat there with tears in his eyes, I asked if he would like to have a Bible study. He agreed, so I found someone from the church and we set up a Bible study with him. I told the devil, "That's one, four more." I walked to the other side of the concession stand, the door opened, and a woman came over to me crying. She explained how she had heard my conversation with Stephen, and wondered if she too could have a Bible study. She told me of her recent divorce and her need of help. Again, another Bible study was set up. I was on a roll and the anointing was all over me. I was so excited I went looking for the third soul.

He was pushing his children on some swings when I spotted him. As I headed in his direction, the Holy Ghost checked me, telling me he had some questions that needed answering. I confronted him and told him that I was a missionary, and that God had told me he needed some questions answered. As the words left my mouth, he fell to his knees and started crying, saying, "About three weeks ago some Mormons came to my house and confused me. While that man [Reverend Libby] was preaching, I asked God to send someone to me to answer my questions."

When Reverend Libby gave the altar call, I took him to the altar area where he repented and a few minutes later received the Holy Ghost.

Needless to say, I was beside myself. I was so excited I went looking for my next two souls. I had the devil on the run and was enjoying the feeling. I was three for three and looking to make it five for five.

When everyone was leaving the park, I still needed two more souls. I did not see anyone who looked anything like a sinner. As I was leaving the park area, I spotted a man and woman sitting in their car. They had been watching and listening to the park service. I gently tapped on the passenger's window and smiled. The woman rolled down the window and I introduced myself, saying, "Hi, I'm Danny Aber, a missionary to Panama, and I would like to invite you to chu...."

She interrupted me excitedly, yelling, "Does your wife have red hair?"

"Yes, she does. Why?" I asked.

With a shocked look on her face, she replied, "She just came by and invited us to church also. I just told my husband that if one more person asked us to church, we were going."

They came during our missionary service and both went to the altar and repented of their sins. I do not know if they ever received the Holy Ghost, but God had begun a work in their lives.

Sometimes I may not have one positive response and at other times one or two out of the five are interested, but this time I was five for five. It came at the right time during our deputation as we were nearing the end of some long traveling days. I had tremendous success after that bout with the devil. The devil gave me a good vacation after that one. All I could say was,

"Thank you, devil, five souls."

7

His Harvest

atthew 9:37-38, *"Then saith he unto his disciples, The harvest truly is plenteous, but the labourers are few; Pray ye therefore the Lord of the harvest, that he will send forth labourers into his harvest."*

John 4:35, *"Say not ye, There are yet four months, and then cometh harvest? behold, I say unto you, Lift up your eyes, and look on the fields; for they are white already to harvest."*

If you are going to be a soul winner, you must understand which harvest God is talking about.

We are always looking for something new to motivate our people to go out and witness. We have seminars, evangelists, and promotions. We give away four-wheelers, deer rifles, and other things to encourage evangelism. When in reality, Jesus gave us the answer: His harvest.

There are two types of harvest fields. One is our harvest, and the other is God's harvest.

When God saves us He makes drastic changes in our lives and the people we affect the most is our families and close friends. If we do not convert them within the first few months of our conversion, it usually takes a long time to witness their personal Pentecost. This is when most everyone makes the "big mistake." They get obsessed with their family or close friends being saved and all they do is focus on them. They usually end up arguing with them about which church is right, or some other topic that their family does not understand, because they have not experienced the saving grace of God. Walls are then built up between them and their families which may take years to tear down.

Our families and friends are "our harvest." We must plant the seed, water it, and trust God to give the increase.

I realized that most of my friends in church were going through the motions of soul winning. Some of them would stand up in every service and ask the church to pray for their family. I know there is nothing wrong with praying for friends and families, but I never heard them mention praying for someone else's family.

That is when I understood God's concept of "His Harvest."

I was so excited about reaching God's harvest that as I passed the city limit sign one day, I felt the Spirit of God touch me. I walked to the sign, laid my hands on it and prayed, "God, my family lives in El Campo and here I am in Bay City. I know you have called me to reach these people, so Lord, lead me to other people's mothers, fathers, brothers, sisters, and friends. Lead me to hungry souls. Take me to Your harvest."

God must have heard me because during my first year in church, God gave me 69 souls who were baptized in Jesus' name or received the Holy Ghost. Thirty-nine from the jail and 30 from town. His harvest is truly plenteous.

When I began to reach out to others in God's harvest, there was a six-month period that I had a visitor in every Sunday service. When I learned to weep and cry for mothers, brothers, sisters, and friends of others, God gave the increase in my family and friends. It took about two years, but it happened.

It all started when a friend from high school called me with this great deal that was going to change my life. When he arrived at my house one Saturday morning after driving over 400 miles, he began to tell me about this great insurance plan from A.L. Williams. He was so excited about this ex-football coach and his product that he went on for about 20 minutes. I then interrupted, "I have never heard of A.L. Williams, or his insurance plan. As a matter of fact, I don't have any insurance, but I can tell you one thing, Parker, I know one greater than A.L. Williams. His name is Jesus Christ. He died for your sins, and He has the best life insurance plan on the market."

He quickly replied, "I'm Baptist."

I responded, "I didn't ask what religion you were, Parker, you need Jesus." I then explained the truth of the one true God and baptism in Jesus' name. He knelt down with me beside the sofa and right there Parker began to ask God to change him. We never spoke about A.L. Williams again that day. I invited Parker to be my special guest the following day at church. We were starting a revival with the Reverend Keith Clark, and I knew God would get ahold of him.

Sunday night, Parker was sitting next to me smelling like Marlboro country, but dressed in a suit. Outside of the smell he could have passed for a church member. Brother Clark walked on the platform about ten minutes into the service and you could tell he was ready to preach.

He spoke of a drunk man who was up and then down, at his wit's end, not knowing what to do next. He then pointed right at Parker and said, "You look like one of us and you are dressed like one of us, but you are not. You look like you have it all together, but your life is really falling apart. You need to repent before your life is completely destroyed."

Needless to say, Parker wasted no time and was the first one to the altar. After he repented, he received the Holy Ghost and was baptized in Jesus' name. After the service Parker told me he had gone through two divorces and was constantly thinking of suicide. He replied, "How did he know what I was going through?"

I smiled and said, "God loved you enough to send you a personal message."

As you can imagine, I was on fire and I was not about to go out. Now my harvest was ready and God was giving the increase.

Parker went back to El Campo that night where his family lived and made a point to see my mother who lived right up the street. He excitedly told her about what had happened to him that night and how the preacher told him exactly what he was thinking.

The last time I had witnessed to my mother, she was sitting in front of the TV crocheting and watching Jimmy Swaggart (with the volume turned down), telling me, "I'm doing all right. I don't hurt anyone. I'm a good person. Someday I might get more involved."

Parker's testimony had an impact on my mother and Wednesday night my mother, little brother and sister came to the revival services. We all sat on the third pew.

Brother Clark announced his sermon that night, "Those That Meant Well."

About halfway through the message he stopped and said, "There is a woman on my right, you mean well, you're always saying that you're going to get right soon, that someday you'll serve the Lord. Well, if you're going to do it, don't be like those who meant well; do it now."

My mother stood up and pushed her way to the middle of the aisle. I honestly thought she was leaving. My little sister and brother were right behind her. When she reached the middle of the aisle she turned to the altar and stopped right in front of the pulpit. She repented of her sins, God filled her with the Holy Ghost, and she was baptized in Jesus' name. When she came out of the water God healed her of scoliosis. She also had been smoking two packs of cigarettes every day for over 20 years. Since that night, she has never touched another one. She has been living for God consistently now for 14 years. She is a member of Brother V.L. Neely's church in Lufkin, Texas.

My little sister and brother received the Holy Ghost and were baptized in Jesus' name, also.

My old roommate, Ben and his wife, Beth, were also added to the church shortly after my mother. They are still living for God and going to the Apostolic Pentecostal Church, with Ben's sister, Marcy, in Bay City, Texas.

I was now able to see my harvest being reaped, but it came after I learned to weep and cry for other people's families and friends. I can truthfully say that it was worth the wait. I feel God gave me my family and friends because I was willing to step into "His Harvest."

While we were in Illinois on deputation some years ago, I was able to visit a friend of mine. I asked about his involvement in soul winning.

He replied, "This is a college town, nobody wants the Holy Ghost. They seem to be interested in everything but God."

I asked him where he worked.

"At the local grocery store," he answered.

I encouraged him to take me there and we would look for a hungry soul. He quickly informed me that he knew everyone there, and that it would be a waste of time to try.

I quickly shot back saying, "God's harvest is plenteous, and besides, you don't know everyone there, but God does."

As we approached the store, I stopped at the front door and began to pray for God to lead me to His harvest. I prayed, "God, I don't know anyone in this store, but You know everyone. I don't know anyone's needs, but You know all of their needs. I'm asking You to lead me to a hungry soul in Your harvest. If there is someone ready right now, let me know, and I'll be faithful to witness to them."

The next few minutes we were walking through the store shopping for things for our meal later that night. We had moved through every aisle without meeting anyone to witness to. As we were preparing to move to the check-out counter, we passed the potato chip section. There was a Frito-Lay man on a small ladder stocking the racks. He was whistling, and having a good time. One would assume by his actions that he was in need of nothing. He seemed to have everything in control. But as I was approaching him, the Holy Ghost spoke to me and said, "He's ready."

My friend looked embarrassed and tried not to stand too close to me. I confronted the Frito-Lay man by asking, "Excuse me, Sir, could you tell me what are the best potato chips to buy?"

He quickly stepped off the ladder to answer this obvious question. "Why, Frito-Lays are the best potato chips!" he boasted.

Tempting him, I shot back, "How do you know Frito's are the best?"

Smiling, he said with confidence, "I've been selling potato chips for eight years. I ought to know what I'm talking about."

"Eight years?" I asked.

"Yeah, eight years," he confirmed.

"Well, if you've been selling potato chips for eight years you sure ought to know what you are talking about. Give me two of your best bags."

He again looked at me and with a sheepish grin, replied, "You're a smart man." He grabbed two king-size bags and placed them in my cart (he must have been working on commission).

As soon as he placed the bags in my cart, I responded, "Now, I want to tell you about the best church in town."

"How do you know it's the best church in town?"

"Because I have been preaching for ten years. I ought to know what I'm talking about."

He hung his head and with a smile he answered, "You got me."

I quickly responded, "You're a smart man."

He asked me where the church was, and I gave him the address.

He smiled and said that he passed by the church everyday on his route.

I asked him if he was married, and he hung his head and tears filled his eyes.

He replied, "My wife left me about five years ago and I don't know where she or my children are now. I just got remarried about a year ago and this marriage is already falling apart. I don't know what to do."

I immediately got his address and phone number and informed him the church was going to call and set up a Bible study. He agreed, giving us the information and right there in God's harvest, a soul was reaped.

Well, if it had been up to me I would have never talked to that man, simply because outwardly he seemed to have everything in his favor. But when you enter into God's harvest, you realize that everyone is a potential candidate to be brought into God's kingdom. Outward circumstances play no part in God's harvest because He looks on the hearts of men.

While finishing up our deputation, I stepped into God's harvest field once again. This time it was in Fresno, California. I was speaking to the ministers of California concerning God's harvest. The hand of the Lord moved on us in a mighty way. After the meeting, we went to Long John Silvers for lunch. As we approached the counter, I noticed that the young woman waiting on us had a tattoo on her hand and looked very distracted. I smiled and joyfully greeted her, saying, "Praise the Lord, Debbie, how are you doing today?"

Shocked, she looked from me to my wife, Lori, and back to me, inquiring, "Do I know you?"

I assured her she did not. So she squinted her eyes and as a puzzling look came over her face, she drilled me, "Then how did you know my name?"

Laughing, I told her I read her name tag. She smiled at my wife and me and said, "I'm so embarrassed."

I then asked her if she had ever heard of the Pentecostal experience.

She said, "No, but I would like to know more about it."

Lori stepped in and began to tell her about the power of God. She was so excited that she promised to go to church with us the following week when we returned to preach at Pastor Vaughn Morton's church.

I know that people always promise you they will come and never do, but when you are in God's harvest, His harvest is always ready.

We arrived in Fresno late that next Sunday afternoon and Lori went straight to Debbie's house to make sure she was coming. She opened the door, dressed and ready to go and it was only four o'clock in the afternoon. She told Lori that she wanted to make sure she was ready, but that there was one small problem.

"My husband is Laotian and he told me he would visit, too, but he wasn't going to attend an American church."

Lori assured her that was fine, but she needed to get her life right first and God would deal with him. About three hours later, Debbie and her little sister were in our missionary service. When I gave the altar call, she literally ran to the altar, weeping and asking God to forgive her. Once again God heard a sinner's request, because she received the Holy Ghost within ten minutes of coming to the altar. It was a wonderful evening.

We were to preach missionary services in two other churches in Fresno. Debbie attended these services with us. Her husband came with her to the last missionary service we held in Fresno.

When I gave the altar call, I noticed Debbie's husband come up to the front. I also noticed a man begin to pray with her husband. Here was this American man talking to a man who did not want to attend an American church. He was laying his hand on his head praying for him. In my mind I thought this guy was going to make Debbie's husband mad, so I walked over and listened to this American man speaking to him. Debbie's husband was shaking his head up and down. The man was the Laotian pastor for Brother Morton's Laotian work! Debbie's husband received the Holy Ghost that night.

God's harvest is plenteous, but it is His labourers who are few.

God knew exactly what He was doing when He directed me to the Long John Silvers. He had a young woman and her Laotian husband who were ready right then.

What were the chances of my speaking in a church with a Laotian pastor in attendance?

I do not know everybody in your city, and neither do you. I do not know every circumstance or situation that is behind each door in your city, and neither do you. But there is a God in heaven who knows every person, circumstance and situation in every city. All God needs is a laborer to take five minutes and step into

HIS HARVEST.

8

Don't Leave Home Without It

merican Express has advertisements all over the world telling people, "Don't leave home without it." Other ads let you know that there is no credit limit with the American Express card.

American Express and the true church should have similar slogans. I am speaking about your personal testimony. It is important to understand that when you leave your house you are always representing Jesus Christ, the church and your pastor, and that the power of your testimony has no limit!

We have all seen the "Footprints in the Sand" poem. I was listening to a woman testify one time, and she was sobbing between every other word. She told us how hard it was for her to live for God, and that she was so depressed that she did not even want to ever leave her house again. Determined not to come to church anymore, she happened to pass that poem which was hanging in the hallway. She read it and started crying again. She thought that if God did not come and pick her up and carry her, she could not make it another step. What a pitiful testimony!

The Bible says that Enoch walked with God and he had this testimony that he pleased God, or in Texas we would say, "He made God happy."

From that day on, I threw my footprints poem away realizing that if I was going to make a difference in this world, I could not sit around waiting on God to come and pick me up, or carry me around. We started a little custom in our house that when we wake up in the mornings we give each other a high-five and say, "Let's make God happy."

It was our way of serving notice to the devil that we were going to walk with God that day.

If you want to make an impact on your community, you have to make God happy by taking your testimony with you. We must start walking with God and quit allowing circumstances to dictate our mood for witnessing or for church attendance. When it comes to your testimony, "Don't leave home without it."

It was a very cold and foggy winter day when I was on my way to preach at the Ramsey Prison Farm in Rosharon, Texas. While driving down Highway 288, a sports car passed me and the driver slammed on his brakes. His car swerved and skidded to a stop. Half of his car was on the road and half was on the shoulder. He then jumped out and ran toward the field to the right of the highway. I had to brake and change lanes to miss crashing into his car. I immediately turned to my wife and told her, "Something's wrong. I'm going back."

I had to travel about one mile farther until I could turn around. As I approached the car in the fog, I saw an emergency vehicle behind the sports car. The driver of the sports car was fighting with the driver of the emergency vehicle. He had pulled his coveralls down over his arms to where he was unable to use them and was hitting him as hard as he could. The man's face was cut and bloody. I stopped my car and told my wife I was going to help the man. I instructed my wife, saying, "If he starts to beat me up, drive off. Don't let him get you."

I then ran as fast as I could. Because he could not see me, I knew I had the advantage. I tackled him and we rolled into the ditch where the grass was about a foot high. The fireman had enough sense to help me. If he had not, I would have been in big trouble. The boy was on dope and he went crazy. He threw me off, and I crawled back on top of him. We repeated this action about four times. Now, I am not going to lie, I was afraid. About the time I thought he was going to whip me and the fireman, a little Mexican man jumped on top of him to help us. We were able to turn him over on his belly and the Mexican man tied the young boy's feet. Looking up at us, he then smiled and said in his broken English, "I can't stay. I'm illegal."

Every muscle in my body was quivering and I was praying, "Oh God! Don't let this guy get up." I grabbed two hands full of his afro and laid on top of his head and shoulders. He began to hyperventilate, and he finally turned his head to the side and began to scream, "Help me. I'm in hell!"

When the boy's face was against the ground, the fireman decided it was his turn now. He started hitting him as hard as he could. After the third hit, I leaned back over his face refusing to let the fireman hit him any more.

The fireman went ballistic hollering, "I'll kill him! That's what I'll do."

By this time, a seventy-year-old man stopped to help. We had him under control, and I was praising God. The fireman stood on the boy's back and leaned into his car reaching for his radio. He called the police and in about five minutes, three Houston police cars were there. They handcuffed the boy and threw him over the trunk of a police car. We were all standing there talking when the policeman asked the bloody fireman, "Are you all right?"

The young boy, who was obviously on drugs, lifted his head and told the policeman, "Yeah, I'm all right."

The policeman went wild, screaming, "I was not asking you, I could care less about you. I'm going to throw you so far in jail you'll never get out. Do you hear me boy?"

The policeman who was writing the report talked to the fireman and then to the old man that had stopped to help. I noticed he looked familiar, so I looked at his name tag. It said, "Calhoun." I could not believe it! This guy was from Bay City, and I had lived with him for about two months. We drank beer, smoked dope, and went to rock concerts 11 years earlier. I had not seen him since God had changed me, but here we were on the side of Highway 288. When he turned to me to take the report, he shook his head in disbelief, asking, "Danny, is that you?"

I responded, "Yes, it's me."

"What are you doing here?" he asked.

I told him I was a preacher and explained what happened. He was amazed. He kept telling the other policeman, "I can't believe Aber is a preacher. He was the biggest troublemaker of them all!"

There I was standing on the side of the highway, my pants torn, tie mangled, and my shirt ripped and dirty. I did not really know why I had stopped, and after grabbing that guy I was really wondering why. But God knew what He was doing, because for the next 30 to 45 minutes, I stood there giving my testimony to three Houston policeman. One of them was an old friend whom I had not seen since I received the Holy Ghost. I am just glad that when I woke up that Sunday morning, "I didn't leave home without it."

Upon our arrival in Panama as missionaries, we were in search of furniture for our house. We would get the military newspaper and go through it looking for a good buy.

Lori called this one family about a dining room table and was told to come over and take a look at it. She picked up her purse along with her personal testimony and off to Fort Howard she went. She was met by a Colombian woman who had married a Puerto Rican serviceman. She invited Lori in, and they began to talk. Lori told her that we were missionaries and that we had just arrived in the country. She asked with what denomination, and Lori told her we were with the United Pentecostal Church.

With a puzzled look on her face, she replied, "I think I went there once and received the Holy Ghost, but my husband would not let me go back."

As tears filled her eyes, Lori started praying for her right there in her home. Her husband, who had been listening from the next room, joined them and apologetically agreed to allow her to go to church with us. About two weeks later, Eddie came with Patricia and they were both filled with the Holy Ghost and were baptized in the name of Jesus. About three months later, Eddie's mother came for a visit from Puerto Rico, and she also received the Holy Ghost and was baptized in Jesus' name. I know of three people who were glad that Lori Aber did not leave home without her personal testimony.

Lori later called another number in the paper looking for a bicycle for our son, Ryan. As the conversation started, the young woman asked where Lori was from, and why she was in Panama. Lori told her that we were missionaries. She began to explain her situation of how she was attending an Assembly of God church and wanted to be baptized. The pastor gave her a book with all the Scriptures on baptism and told her to study it thoroughly. She did and went back, ready to be baptized.

He explained how he was going to do it, saying, "I will dunk you three times in the name of the Father, and of the Son, and of the Holy Ghost."

Celina stopped him, and insisted, "That's not what the Bible says. I'm supposed to be baptized in Jesus' name!"

Mad and frustrated the pastor told her to find another church.

She then explained how she was searching for a church that baptized in Jesus' name. She then asked Lori, "Do you know anyone who would baptize me in Jesus' name?"

Lori was ecstatic, and said, "That's how we baptize. Where do you live? My husband and I will come by and have a Bible study with you."

She gave Lori the directions to her house, and it turned out to be only three blocks from our church. Celina received the Holy Ghost and was baptized in Jesus' name. Thank God, again, Lori Aber did not leave home without it.

While in Pomeroon, Guyana, which is an Amerindian Village, God performed a miracle. I was there setting up some services in the river areas and we came down to Charity (a small town on the river) for some supplies. Feeling the anointing of God, I was witnessing and telling everyone I met about my personal testimony. While I was talking, a young man ran up to me crying, "Are you the missionary, the owner of the big van?"

When I asked why, he told us his daughter was ill with malaria and was going to die if proper attention was not given to her. I was expected to be in a service with 80 people in about an hour, and I knew I could not leave, so I asked him where his daughter was. He pointed to the local hospital.

I walked to the hospital with him and two of my young ministers. I asked the details of her condition. He said she had been sick for about three weeks, but her condition had worsened two days earlier. The doctor said he had done all he could do for her and that she needed emergency help.

Her father pleaded, "Pastor, you're the only one with a vehicle. Will you please help me?"

Upon arriving at the two-room hospital, we encountered five other malaria patients. I was taken to the young girl and prayed that God would heal her. She was burning up with fever when we started praying, but as soon as I anointed her with oil, the fever left. She sat up in bed and asked for something to eat. Thirty minutes later, she was walking down the road with us, completely healed, as her father was praising God. He asked the pastor in that area if he would come and hold a Thanksgiving service at his house about an hour up the river. From that miracle a preaching point was born, a girl was healed, and two young ministers learned a very important lesson. No matter where you are, how you feel, or what you are doing, when it comes to your testimony,

don't leave home without it!

9

The Need of Divine Help

Superman was walking through the streets with his hands in his pockets, head down, seemingly unaware of the danger approaching his city. He was oblivious to the screams, looks of fear and horror on the faces of the people. He had been knocked on the head and had amnesia. The people were running through the street screaming and hollering, "Somebody save us! Help! Where's Superman?"

As you turned the page in the comic book, the bomb was getting closer and the faces of the people were more terrified. Again the people were screaming, "Please, somebody help us."

There was Superman in the midst of the turmoil, unaware of who he was. He had the power to save his people and his city, but he did not know who he was.

Turning the page again, the bomb was now closer and the people more frantic. A group of crazed people pushed Clark Kent (Superman) from behind and he was unable to get his hands out of his pant's pockets and he fell and bumped his head on the ground. He rose up, shook his head and heard the same screams, that up to a few seconds earlier, he had been oblivious to. Seeing the bomb approaching, he jumped into a phone booth, burst out as Superman, and caught the bomb right before it hit the city. He then carried it out over the ocean and dropped it in as it harmlessly exploded. Superman had saved his people and his city.

I had to stop and laugh as this comic book reminded me of the church. We walk through our cities unaware of who we really are. We pass people everyday, never looking in their terrified faces. We never see the fear in their eyes because we have forgotten who we really are. We walk with our heads down trying to make it through another day. We have forgotten that we have the power to save our cities. While the world is screaming for help, we wander through life like Superman with amnesia.

The woman whose husband has left her, the man whose wife has been unfaithful, the children who have seen the horrors of divorce and broken homes, the teenager who has tried drugs or alcohol for the first time, the young teenagers who have lost their virginity or the elderly who no one has time for, all of them have "need of divine help."

I hope this chapter is able to shake you or wake you, so that, like Superman, you will come to yourself, realize who you really are and arise with the power God has given you to save your city.

"Lift up your eyes and look on the fields for they are white already to harvest." Every day people pass you wondering if there is anybody who can help them.

Banks can put shoes on their feet, a robe on their back, and a ring on their finger, but they cannot take the lost out of their soul. Look at those around you. They have "need of divine help."

About 14 years ago, God awoke me from a sound sleep at two o'clock in the morning. Sitting up on the edge of the bed wide awake, I felt the Holy Ghost quicken me to pray for my wife's sister, Robin. We were in Bay City, Texas, and Robin was living in Iowa, but the Holy Ghost quickened me to pray for her right then. I went into the living room and started praying. A spirit of intercession consumed me, and I prayed until around six o'clock. I told my wife, Lori, that God had awakened me to pray for Robin. About 6:30 that morning we received a phone call from Lori's mother telling us that Robin had been in an automobile accident about two o'clock that morning, and that the doctors and highway patrolmen could not believe that she had survived. God touched Robin because she only suffered bruises and no broken bones.

The car was totaled and after seeing the pictures of the wreck, one would not believe she had lived and lived without serious injury. I feel that in the moment of her "need of divine help" God supplied her with an intercessor.

Robin is now living in Lake Jackson, Texas. She is full of the Holy Ghost, married and has three children.

While in Panama as a missionary, I was in the church office praying for God to lead me to hungry souls. I heard a knocking sound and went to the door. There was a young man standing there, obviously on drugs. He was unshaven and his eyes were glazed over as he stood there asking to talk with me. My first response was to tell him to leave, but God quickened to me my prayer of desiring to meet hungry souls. I quickly opened the door and invited him into my office to talk.

He introduced himself, "I'm John Williams, and I need to tell you about my past."

I shook his hand and said, "I'm Pastor Aber, and I don't want to hear about your past. I'm going to tell you about your future."

I taught John the *Eight Steps to Life* Bible study and after about two hours in the Word of God, John's eyes lit up as he saw that Jesus was God. He looked me straight in the eyes and said, "I want to repent, right now."

For the next hour, John was pouring his heart out in repentance. God must have heard him because he received the Holy Ghost in my office.

The young man who knocked on the church door glassy eyed and high on drugs was now talking correctly, and his eyes were crystal clear.

I drove him to the area where he lived, and when I stopped on a side road, he pointed to a house (small wooden box) on top of a mountain. "That's my house," he said.

I reminded him of the church service the next night, and he promised to be there.

We started the Wednesday night Bible study with prayer. During the worship service, John, his wife, and two children came in. Thinking that John would stand up and testify, I asked if anyone had a testimony. To my surprise his wife jumped up first. I had no idea what she would say, so I downed my head expecting the worst. She stood up and started crying. I raised my head and looked into the eyes of a sincere woman. She said, "I don't know what you did to my husband yesterday, but he came home for the first time in five days. He had a smile on his face and he hugged me and apologized, asking me to forgive him. He then told me to take the children outside so he could pray. After about an hour he came out and told me to go and pray while he watched the children. Like I said, I don't know what you did to him, but I want to thank you because now I have a husband and my children have a father. Whatever he has, I want it, and I want it tonight!"

Lucy received the Holy Ghost that night, and I baptized John and Lucy in the wonderful name of Jesus. When I left Panama to work in Guyana, John was attending Bible school and felt his call to preach.

God took what seemed to be a hopeless situation and made it right. A man who was a drug addict and neglecting his family had finally found an inner peace. He was one of the many people who we pass every day who was in "need of divine help." Had I looked on the outward, I would have chased him away that day, but instead God found a vessel ready for the Master's use.

Not long after John and Lucy were converted, I was preaching about soul winning. I told the church that if we would enter into intercessory prayer, God would bring sinners in off the streets. About the same time, the back door of the church opened and a tall black man walked in. For some reason when

I saw him, I knew he was an American. After the service, I went and shook his hand and spoke in English to him. He looked rather puzzled and asked, "Why did you speak in English to me? You didn't know I was an American." I replied, "I just knew." I then led him to my office where he began to tell me about how bad he had it. I stopped him, and God quickened me to give him my testimony. I told him of my problems of drugs, alcohol, and that I had even tried to commit suicide. When I said that, he dropped his head and the tears began to flow. He rolled up his shirt sleeves and on his wrists were recent cuts from a failed suicide. He told me that he had just left the hospital and something had told him to come in and speak to me. He was another person we pass everyday who was in "need of divine help."

Bernie never allowed God to help him. He rejected the truth God brought his way, but God's Word does not come back void. Bernie lived in San Miguelito, which was one of the worst sections in Panama. Bernie was an American living in an apartment complex nine stories high. He was on the top floor, 99 steps up and the building had no elevator. Each section had two apartments.

About 11:30 one night, I received a phone call from a young woman who was very upset. She was crying and saying, "I need help. I need someone to talk to."

She was an American who had married a Panamanian. I asked her how she knew to call me, and she said that her neighbor, Bernie, gave her my number, and told her that I really cared about people. Lori and I went and talked with Nicky that night, and as she poured her heart out to us, we realized that we had found someone else who had "need of divine help."

Nicky came to church the next Sunday morning and received the Holy Ghost. Pastor Sandy from Mississippi was preaching and after the service, Nicky was baptized in Jesus' name in the Panama Canal. She has sold out to God, and He has blessed her. She has already won some of her family members to the Lord. What Bernie turned down, Nicky received.

We need to understand that every person God places in our path is in

"NEED OF DIVINE HELP."

10

Just Do It

It was in the year of 1993, I was a missionary in Panama, and things were not going well for me physically. I had been sick for some time, and I was really discouraged. In spite of the souls who were being won and miracles that were taking place, I was at my lowest point. I was very sick when I finally decided to go see a doctor. As I was sitting in the waiting room, I was thinking, "Something bad is wrong with me. Cancer, sugar diabetes or maybe a heart problem. Whatever it is, it's bad." I was seen by the doctor, and when I told him my father died at the age of 46 of a heart attack, he looked concerned. He sent me to a clinic for several tests and told me to return the next day.

That night was very stressful. I was wondering if I had enough insurance to sustain my family in case of my death, and I was worried about what my children were going to do. Was my wife going to have to work a double shift at a Shoney's after I was gone? It was a terrible night. After waking up the next morning, I was the first one waiting outside the doctor's office. When they opened the doors, I walked in prepared for bad news. I was mentally ready for whatever the doctor had to tell me, or so I thought.

I was called into his office. While he was reading the test results, he had a very disturbed look on his face. It was just as I had supposed; it was something bad. He looked up at me and asked if my wife was with me. My heart almost stopped. I thought to myself, "It must be more serious than I thought."

I told him I was alone, and he said, "I think you need to go and get her, and meet me back in my office at two o'clock. I would like to speak to both of you."

I was devastated. I went straight home and sat Lori down and told her that the doctor wanted to see both of us together. A worried look overtook her face. She asked, "Did he say what was wrong?"

"No," I replied, and she immediately started crying and praying.

We met the doctor at two o'clock sharp. He asked us to sit down. I was clutching my wife's hand, knowing that the news was going to shatter her. He looked up at us as I was preparing myself for the news of cancer or some other major problem.

But he just calmly said, "Mrs. Aber, your husband has a serious problem."

Here it comes, I thought, Lori is going to fall apart.

He said, "Sobre peso."

When he said that, Lori literally fell out of her chair laughing so hard she could hardly catch her breath. She asked the doctor, "Sobre peso?"

The doctor responded with a smile, "That's right, sobre peso."

Being interpreted, "overweight," or in other words, "I'm fat."

Well, I am not going to lie, I did not quite see the humor in what he was saying. I mean, I was prepared for cancer, heart disease, or diabetes, but not for being overweight. He said I was fat. "That's it? Fat, nothing else?" I questioned.

"That's right, nothing else. You just need to lose weight," he instructed.

A few hours later, I decided to go to the El Dorado Mall and walk around. I needed to get my head on straight. After all, that was quite a large pill to swallow.

I knew the doctor was right, and I had to deal with it. As I was browsing, I passed a sport's store and there in the window was a T-shirt that had the slogan across the front, "Just Do It!"

I stood there looking at that T-shirt and made up my mind right then. I would just do it. I went in and bought the T-shirt, a pair of warm-ups, and some new jogging shoes. From that day on for the next six months I ate correctly, walked, exercised everyday, and without any type of gimmick, I lost over 55 pounds.

I just did it.

Every time I come back to the States it seems there is a new gimmick out there to lose weight. I remember the "Cambridge Diet" and then there was the "Herbal Life" craze. Then along came the "Delta Diet."

I was at one church and they were into selling the "Delta Diet." They told me I had to buy it, because I could not lose weight without it. The pastor told me I needed not one box, but two. I asked how much and he told me, "Only $80 dollars." I wrote the check out and was on my way to being lean and mean again. About two months later, the pastor saw me and asked, "How much did you lose?"

I declared, "All I lost was $80 dollars."

Another time I came back to the States, people were selling these diet cookies. You were to eat one cookie and drink about a gallon of coffee. It would swell in your stomach and give you that "filled up feeling." All it did for me was make me feel like the Goodyear blimp.

And then our most recent diet gimmick "Formula One." Now it is beyond me why they named it Formula One, because they tell you to take three (not one) of them babies at 10:00 am and three (not one) more at 3:00 pm. You would then be too wired to eat anything until about two o'clock in the morning, because that is about the time you come down to get ready for bed.

What I am really trying to say is that no matter what diet gimmick is sold or offered on the market, the only true way to lose weight and keep it off is to "Just Do It!"

But to take it another step farther, the same principle has to be applied to soul winning. No matter what gimmick someone comes up with, or what idea a preacher has, or what evangelism tool is developed, the only way you will ever win a soul is if you "Just Do It!"

When I decided that I was going to be a soul winner, my pastor told me, "Don't tell me; show me."

Theodore Roosevelt said, "Whenever you are asked if you can do a job, tell 'em, 'Certainly, I can!' — and get busy and find out how to do it."

When I started the jail ministry, I didn't go to a seminar or buy a $20 syllabus. I simply "Just did it."

Ed Depiso was sitting in the county jail when I met him. I was preaching when he yelled, "Shut up! I don't want to hear about your God. I'm an atheist. Why don't you prove your God is real?"

Amazed at the question, I replied, "Right now?"

He responded, "Yes, right now."

I smiled and said, "Okay, I'll prove my God is real." Upon my reply, about 12 men came out of their cells to see how I was going to prove that my God was real. I asked if they were ready and the atheist retorted, "Yes, we're ready."

I said, "All right, I'm going to prove it right now."

It was rather funny because you could have heard a pin drop. They all seemed to lean forward in expectation of hearing my reply. I then boasted, "You're in there, and I'm out here." Pausing for several minutes to allow that thought to sink in, I then continued, "I'd like to stay, but I can't. They used to let me stay here, but not anymore. I can only stay for two hours and then I have to leave. I'm going home in my car, to my wife, and she is going to have a nice meal waiting. My son will run and jump in my lap and try to tell me what he has been doing, and then we are all going to go to church to worship a real God."

Looking at my watch, I continued, "As a matter of fact, my time is up and because my God is real, I'm leaving. Would any of you like to go with me? Oh! I forgot your God's not real. You have to stay here, so I'll see you next week."

I walked out praising the Lord all the way home.

On Wednesday, about 5:30 in the evening, I was getting ready for church when I received a phone call from the sheriff's department. They told me a young man had just been released from jail and he was caught hitchhiking. This was against the law and when they picked him up, he told them to call me. Because they knew that I worked with the prisoners, they decided to call and see if I was going to go and get him, or if I wanted them to pick him back up. I assured them that I was on my way. Well, you can imagine the look on my face when I pulled up beside that young man standing on the side of Highway 35. He was the atheist in the jail that Sunday who challenged me to prove my God was real. As he climbed into my car, I introduced myself, "Hi, I'm Danny Aber."

He quickly responded, "I know. We talked about you in the jail and a guy gave me your card. I'm Ed Depiso."

I stopped and bought him something to eat and headed for the house. I told him we were on our way to church and I wanted him to come. He shook his head and mumbled, "I'm an atheist."

"Well, then you don't have anything to worry about," I said smiling. I gave him some clean clothes and off to church we went. Pastor Moore was teaching about the One True God. As he taught, Ed rubbed his chest with both hands. The more Pastor taught, the more he rubbed his chest. When the altar call was given, Ed looked at me crying and said, "God's real. I know He's real. I can feel Him." After going to the altar, Ed repented of all his sins, and God proved how real He really was. When the Holy Ghost fell on him, he danced and shouted for at least 45 minutes and then he was baptized in Jesus' name.

I took him home to his wife that night and explained to her what had happened. She started crying and told me, "I was raised in an old Assemblies of God church, and when I was a little girl I received the Holy Ghost and I never have forgotten it. I know God wants us to get our lives right with Him."

The following Sunday night, Ed's wife was refilled with the Holy Ghost and was baptized in Jesus' name. After her baptismal, they asked Pastor Moore to renew their marriage vows. God did a wonderful work in both of their lives.

Four days later, Ed was back in jail. There was an outstanding warrant for his arrest in Indiana, so the sheriff's department picked him back up. When I got there Sunday, Ed had already prayed three through to the Holy Ghost and had all of them ready for the preaching. That afternoon a man named Jim, who was sentenced to 30 years in prison for murder, received the Holy Ghost.

Ed told me what had happened, and that he knew God had put him back in there to show them that my God was real. After all, a week earlier he had been boasting of being an atheist. He told me that his parents had just arrived from Philadelphia and they were at the Oasis Motel. He asked me to go and tell them about Jesus. After leaving the jail, I went straight to their room and knocked on the door. A short man about five foot tall answered the door with a smile on his face.

I introduced myself saying, "Hi, I'm Danny Aber, from the United Pentecostal Church."

He interrupted excitedly, "I'm Ed Depiso, my son has told me so much about you. I want to thank you, your church and the pastor for everything you guys have done to help my son."

I quickly responded, "That's good, but what you need to do is come to church."

Smiling from ear to ear, he replied, "I'd be glad to go."

Surprised at his quick response, I felt bad because it was so easy. I felt like I needed to explain to him we were Pentecostal. I told him, "Mr. Depiso, we're Pentecostal and we...."

He interrupted me, patting me on the shoulder, declaring, "I know all about church, I'm a church-going man. I have been Catholic for 68 years, all my life."

I thought, "Oh, boy, a Catholic in a Pentecostal service on a Sunday night; he just thinks he knows what church is all about."

Church started and no Depisos. Lori was in the choir. When I saw her smile about midway through the second congregational song, I turned around and saw them moving into the third pew from the back. I grabbed my Bible and took a seat by Mr. Depiso. I immediately stood up and started worshiping God and clapping my hands. I saw something move out of the corner of my eye. Mr. Depiso was standing beside me clapping his hands. I lifted my hands, praising God. Again I saw something move. There he was, with his hands raised, crying, talking to God.

After the preaching, I told him he needed to repent. When I showed him in the Bible where repentance was necessary, he told me, "If that's what the Bible says, I must do it. How do I repent?"

"Let's go up front to the altar and you can repent," I instructed. Turning to the altar I walked to the front of the church, Mr. Depiso following me. I stopped at the first pew, turned and looked at Mr. Depiso who had both his hands raised, weeping and crying, asking God to forgive him. His wife was right beside him weeping and repenting also.

After 20 minutes of earnest repenting, Mr. Depiso started jumping up and down, shouting all over the front of the church. He was speaking in tongues, full of the Holy Ghost. His wife was standing there watching with a puzzled look on her face. I then informed Mr. Depiso that since he had repented and received the Holy Ghost, he now needed to be baptized in Jesus' name. He looked at me through tear-soaked eyes and asked, "Is that what the Bible says?"

I answered, "Yes, sir, that's what the Bible says."

Turning to the Scriptures, I showed him Acts 2:38; 8:16; 10:48; 19:5.

He then proclaimed, "I want to be baptized right now in Jesus' name!"

His wife spoke up saying, "If you baptize him, you're going to baptize me, too."

Pastor Moore had both of them in the baptismal tank together, when he asked, "Who wants to be first?"

Mrs. Depiso spoke up saying, "Let my husband go first."

When Mr. Depiso came out of the water he was speaking in tongues and throwing water everywhere. But the best part was, his wife literally pushed him out of the way shouting, "BAPTIZE ME NOW! I WANT THE HOLY GHOST!"

Mrs. Depiso came out of the water speaking in tongues, full of the Holy Ghost. Her testimony later that night was, "I hope there is a church like this in Philadelphia. I have never felt this good in my whole life."

All it takes is for someone to "Just Do It!"

I don't have a $20 syllabus to sell you that will make you the next "super soul winner of Pentecost."

I have no profound words of knowledge, no promotions, such as shopping carts full of groceries, four-wheelers, books on approaches to get your foot in the door, nor an Amway meeting for contacts to try and hype you up on soul winning.

John Wooden said, "Do not let what you cannot do interfere with what you can do."

All I can say is, you can do it! His harvest is plenteous. Just be yourself, walk into His harvest and

"Just Do It!"